New Hampshire's Parklands

A Guide to Public Parklands in The Granite State

by
Bruce Sloane

Published for
the New Hampshire Division of Parks and Recreation

by
Peter E. Randall
PUBLISHER

Additional copies available from
New Hampshire Division of Parks and Recreation
Post Office Box 856, Concord, NH 03301

or from Peter E. Randall Publisher
Post Office Box 4726, Portsmouth, NH 03801

Library of Congress Cataloging-in-Publication Data

Sloane, Bruce, 1935 –
  New Hampshire's parklands.

  Includes index.
  1. Parks — New Hampshire — Guide-books.
  2. Historic sites — New Hampshire — Guide-books.
  3. New Hampshire — Description and travel —
  1981 –   — Guide-books. I. Title.
  F32.3.S56 1985   917.42′0443   85-19146
  ISBN 0-914339-08-7

Wallis Sands State Beach, George Sylvester photograph.

New Hampshire's Parklands

Small waterfall at the Flume, George Sylvester photograph.

Contents

Foreword

Experience New Hampshire!

New Hampshire's Parklands introduces you to one of the finest collections of public park properties in America. From the ¾ million-acre White Mountain National Forest hiker's mecca to 5-acre historic Fort Stark on the rock-bound Atlantic coast, our public parks and recreation areas provide unrivalled opportunities for outdoor recreation, historic appreciation, or just casual sight-seeing.

A visit to one of our mountain top alpine gardens, or to the driftwood graveyards of our expansive ocean beaches is guaranteed to be a memorable family experience! Skiing, camping, swimming, hiking, and fishing, in the same great outdoors that molded a young Daniel Webster's eloquence and inspired a young Robert Frost's poetry, are but a small taste of what New Hampshire public parks are all about. You haven't really experienced New Hampshire until you visit our unique collection of historic sites.

Catch the New Hampshire of yesterday against the harpsichord background and musical touching of goblets raised to the King at our 280 year old colonial governor's mansion in Portsmouth. Visit "Aspet," the first historic property in the National Park system to be devoted to an artist: the Saint-Gaudens memorial site on the Connecticut River is filled with the treasures of this great American sculptor. And see the farm where Robert Frost wrote: "Just specimens is all New Hampshire has, one each of everything in a showcase, which naturally she doesn't care to sell."

Over the years we've assembled this collection of specimens — not for sale — but for you to enjoy! I hope you will use *New Hampshire's Parklands* not only as your guide to our public park showcase, but also as a small sampler of what New Hampshire has to offer.

John H. Sununu
Governor

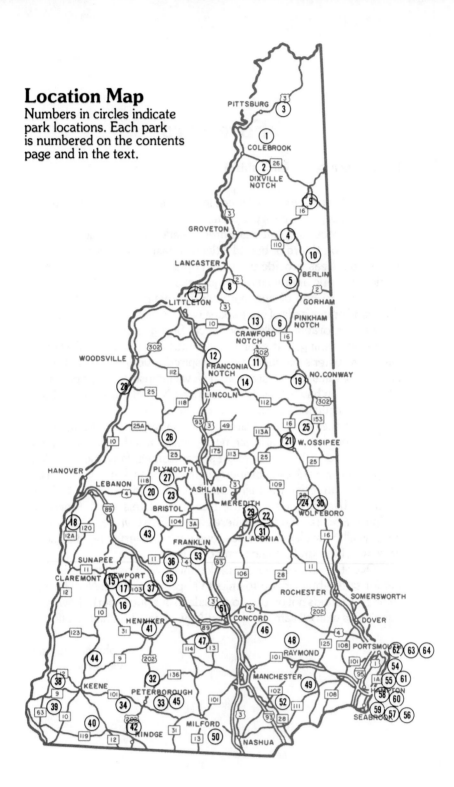

Location Map
Numbers in circles indicate park locations. Each park is numbered on the contents page and in the text.

PITTSBURG ③

① COLEBROOK

② 26 DIXVILLE NOTCH

⑨

GROVETON

④ 110

⑩

LANCASTER ⑤ BERLIN

⑧ 2 GORHAM

⑦ LITTLETON 3

⑬ ⑥ PINKHAM NOTCH

CRAWFORD NOTCH 16

WOODSVILLE 302 ⑫ 302 ⑪ FRANCONIA NOTCH

⑳ 25 ⑭ NO. CONWAY

LINCOLN

⑯ 153 ㉕ W. OSSIPEE

㉑

HANOVER ㉖ PLYMOUTH ㉗ ASHLAND ㉒ WOLFEBORO

LEBANON ⑳ ㉓ BRISTOL MEREDITH ㉔ ㉚

⑱ ㊸ FRANKLIN ㉙ ㉒ ㉛ LACONIA

SUNAPEE ㊱ ㊳ NEWPORT ⑮ ⑰ ㊲ ROCHESTER SOMERSWORTH

CLAREMONT ⑯ ㉟ DOVER

⑯ ㊶ HENNIKER ⑤¹ CONCORD ㊻ PORTSMOUTH ㉒ ㉓ ㉔

㊹ RAYMOND ㊽ ⑤⁴ ⑤⁵ ㉖¹

⑱ ㉜ KEENE PETERBOROUGH ㉝ ㊺ MANCHESTER ㊾ ⑤⁸ ⑥⁰

㊴ ㉞ ⑤² ⑤⁹ ㊼ ㊶ SEABROOK

㊵ ㊷ RINDGE MILFORD ㊿ NASHUA

Introduction

The year 1985 is the 50th anniversary of New Hampshire's state parks. The state is blessed with natural beauty, from lofty mountains and rocky notches to a seacoast both sandy and rugged. Scattered through the state are thousands of streams and brooks, gleaming lakes, and acres of forests. New Hampshire's rich historical background stretches back more than 300 years, to pre-colonial days.

Preserving that heritage are more than 70 state parks, historical sites, beaches, wayside parks, and natural areas, plus federal properties of the White Mountain National Forest and Saint-Gaudens National Historic Site, and a county recreation area. In addition to providing four-season recreation, the parks increase our appreciation and knowledge of the natural world, and enhance our cultural background.

In New Hampshire parks you can gaze at the world-famous Old Man of the Mountain, visited by some 2,000,000 people yearly. You can reach the summit of Mount Washington, highest peak in the northeastern United States, or ascend scores of lesser mountains. You can go up and down the mountains by foot, tramway, ski lift, or car. You can swim in a mountain lake, and dip into the ocean surf. You can examine the delicate shore ecology, and see acres of rhododendron blossoms. You can visit the former homes, farms, and mansions of both well-known and little-known New Hampshire poets, orators, politicians, and pre-revolutionary governors. You can examine unique geologic glacial lakes, mini-canyons, and boulders.

Whatever you want to do — swim or snowmobile, hike or sightsee, fish or camp, climb a cliff, investigate a wildflower trail, or just lie in the sun—New Hampshire's parks have something to offer.

The parks also preserve and protect. Many have extensive wilderness areas, virgin stands of timber, or natural shore areas. As New Hampshire has grown, many of its parks have been threatened by lumbering, commercial exploitation, proposed highways, or similar developments. And many have been saved for the public through arduous, long, and expensive negotiations.

Much of the credit for preserving this heritage belongs to the Society for the Protection of New Hampshire Forests. Since its founding in 1901 the Society has been instrumental in purchasing land for parks, lobbying for their preservation, and providing educational materials and forums for discussion.

Overseeing this heritage is the New Hampshire Division of Parks and Recreation. Increasing demands and limited resources place the Division on a knife edge balancing act: the parks must be protected and preserved, but the increasing demands of the public must be recognized. And, although parks must be available and provide for today's recreation, they must be maintained for the generations that come after us. Conservation in its broadest sense means "wise use." Only through wise use can the state keep its scenic spendor and natural beauty.

At the dedication of the Sherman Adams Summit Building on the top of Mount Washington in September, 1980, the late Governor Hugh J. Gallen summed up the state's responsibilities: "We in the public sector have legal control over the operation and maintenance of these facilities. But we are merely custodians of the land, the rivers and streams that, in the final analysis, are owned not by the government but rather by the people of the state."

Enjoy New Hampshire's state parks, Whether you come for a few hours or a few weeks, whether you come from Manchester, Keene, Boston, or Los Angeles, enjoy the parks. Use them wisely, and take care of them for those who will come after you.

Types of Parks

Although the term "park" is used in a general sense, there are several types of areas covered:

- *State Parks.* These areas have extensive facilities for visitors, appropriate to the activities of the park. Most feature a multitude of different activities, such as swimming, hiking, camping, skiing, or nature walks.
- *State Beaches.* Swimming and other water activities, either fresh water or ocean, are the major features. Bathhouses and related facilities are available.
- *Natural Areas.* These preserve natural features of geological or biological interest. Although some have extensive facilities for visitors, most have a "wilderness" appeal.
- *Wayside Parks.* Usually set in a scenic location, these are roadside picnic sites, with facilities adequate for the activity.
- *Historic Sites.* Historic sites preserve the cultural or historical heritage of New Hampshire. Visitor facilities vary.
- *Others.* This includes a federally-operated national forest, historic sites, and wildlife refuge, and county recreation areas operated by county government.

Fees, Camping and Regulations

About half the areas have an admission or day use fee, and all parks with camping facilities charge for their use. If a park has a fee, it is noted in the description. Since charges are subject to change, exact fees are not quoted.

Day use fees (in the parks that have them) are charged for each person entering the park. They are quite reasonable, less than half the price of an average movie ticket. Fees are charged only during the main season as indicated for each park, and for some they apply only on weekends and holidays. Children under 12 in family groups are admitted free, and at historic sites children under 18 are admitted free. Dogs are not allowed on beaches, and are permitted in parks only on a leash. Starting in 1986, pets will not be allowed in New Hampshire state parks.

Frequent park users may prefer to purchase discount coupon books or summer season tickets good at all parks. New Hampshire residents age 65 or over are admitted free to all facilities, except aerial rides on weekends. (Bring proper identification.) Special rates apply to organized groups.

Many of the state beaches, particularly along the New Hampshire coast, have fees for parking instead of admission. In summer, visitors pay to ride the Aerial Tramway at Franconia Notch and the Gondola lift at Mount Sunapee.

In winter, skiers pay lift fees at Franconia and Mount Sunapee. The prices are comparable to other ski resorts. Single rides, day, and season passes are available.

Many parks and forests have campgrounds. Some have several hundred sites. Camping fees are charged on a site basis, per night. This means that an entire family will only pay one fee if they use only one site.

This book is arranged by geographic regions. This lets you look over all the attractions in the region of your interest, and helps you pick out parks of interest if you know you will be in a specific region of the state.

For specific fees, regulations, and further information, contact the New Hampshire Division of Parks and Recreation, 105 Loudon Road, P.O. Box 856, Concord, NH 03301.

Friends of the Parks and Volunteers

Like all of us, parks need friends. The Friends of the Parks are non-profit groups that raise money, build trails, prepare exhibits, conduct special programs, or do similar activities for a particular

11

park. These efforts enrich and enhance a visitor's experience.

Some of the parks that have active Friends include Robert Frost, Rhododendron, Wentworth-Coolidge, Odiorne Point, and Weeks. Other Friends groups are forming, or being planned. If you would like to join or form a Friends of the Parks group, or want additional information, contact the Division of Parks and Recreation at the address above.

Individual volunteers can also make a meaningful contribution. Volunteers do a variety of tasks, from maintaining trails to providing visitor information. Most donate an occasional Saturday or weekend, or more time if available. Volunteers with special skills, such as retired teachers, historians, or archaeologists, may give talks or conduct tours in their areas of expertise. For further information, contact the Volunteer Coordinator at the Division of Parks and Recreation.

Information for the Handicapped

Because the state parks have been developed over a period of 50 years, they vary widely in their accessibility to the handicapped. As parks are improved, and new facilities developed, more and more of them will meet current standards of accessibility.

For example, the aerial tramway and summit building and surrounding walkway at Cannon Mountain in Franconia Notch, and the Sherman Adams Summit Building on Mount Washington are totally accessible by wheelchair. Many nature trails are too rugged for wheelchairs, but some are being made accessible. Restroom access varies widely from park to park. Most of the larger parks have handicapped parking areas. A few beach areas have wheelchair ramps, but many that don't are still accessible by wheelchair.

In addition, there are some specific programs for the handicapped. The New England Handicapped Sportsmen's Association conducts ski programs at Franconia Notch and Mount Sunapee. The Mayfest and Oktoberfest festivals for the elderly and handicapped at Mount Sunapee have hosted more than 20,00 people in the 1970s and 1980s. Hospitals, treatment centers, and special schools may have use of the parks at reduced fees when advanced arrangements are made.

For specific information, see "Access to Recreation," an access guide to New Hampshire state parks, available from the Division. Published in 1982, the guide focuses on the facilities and activity areas in the parks, detailing their usability for individuals using wheelchairs.

Fishing along the Androscoggin River, Errol, George Sylvester photograph.

NORTHERN REGION

Coleman State Park, Douglas Armsden photograph.

1 COLEMAN STATE PARK

Stewartstown

Off N.H. Route 26 and an unnumbered road, 12 miles east of Colebrook

The northern corner of New Hampshire is known as the Connecticut Lakes Region. Coleman State Park lies on Little Diamond Pond on the southern edge of this thickly wooded, hilly to mountainous area. The cool lakes are filled with hungry fish, and hunting is popular in the sparsely populated surrounding countryside.

Within the park trout fishing is superb in Little Diamond Pond and in several streams. Small boats are permitted, but speed is restricted. The park is the northern terminal of the Androscoggin Trail, a hiking path 55 miles long that ends in the town of Berlin.

The campground has 30 sites for tent camping, a recreation building, and picnic sites. The season runs from late May to mid-October. A fee is charged for camping.

2 DIXVILLE NOTCH STATE PARK

Dixville

On N.H. Route 26

In the West they are called mountain passes; in the South they are gaps. In New Hampshire they are called notches. And New Hampshire has several — all very scenic.

The town of Dixville is perhaps best known for its early voting — usually first in the nation — in presidential elections. Dixville Notch itself, less than two miles long, is the state's most northern and narrowest mountain notch. Steep grades from both directions lead to a rocky cleft barely wide enough for the two-lane highway. Jagged, near vertical cliffs, shaped by glacial ice, loom up on both sides.

The compact nature of the park makes it easy to visit. Waterfalls tumble down Cascade Brook into a small gorge. Additional waterfalls and rapids lie along Flume Brook. The falls are especially attractive during the spring run-off. Because many of the natural features are close to the road, development has been kept to a minimum.

A hiking trail up Table Rock leads to interesting views of surrounding cliffs. A longer trail up Sanguinary Ridge has long vistas into the mountains of Maine, and also looks down on the Balsams Hotel, a classic mountain resort.

There are two picnic areas along the highway, and an old graveyard. There are no fees.

3 LAKE FRANCIS STATE PARK

Pittsburg

Off U.S. Route 3, 7 miles north of Pittsburg on River Road

Lake Francis is a 2,000 acre man-made lake on the Connecticut River. It lies in the far north wilderness of the state, just south of the river's source, the Connecticut Lakes. It is visited primarily by hunters and fishermen.

This small lake-front park has 40 primitive campsites, a boat launching ramp, and picnic tables. Canoeists often camp here to explore the upper Connecticut area. Rainbow trout, salmon, and pickerel lurk in the cool waters of the lake. Hunting in this spruce- and fir-covered region is good for deer and gamebirds. The park opens in mid-May and remains open through Columbus Day. There is a fee for camping.

4 MILAN HILL STATE PARK

Milan

Off N.H. Route 16, 2 miles west of Milan on N.H. Route 110B

Milan Hill is clustered among the pines, hills, and lakes of northern New Hampshire. Its 37 acres has few crowds. The main feature is the fire tower on top of 1,737-foot high Milan Hill, with sweeping views of southern Canada, the northern White Mountains, and the mountains of Maine.

The wooded campground has 24 primitive campsites. There are some picnic tables, and a playground. Good trout fishing is nearby.

Fees are charged for day visits and camping during the season from late June to September.

5 MOOSE BROOK STATE PARK

Gorham

Off U.S. Route 2, 2 miles west of Gorham

Surrounded by the White Mountains, Moose Brook State Park near Berlin has superb views south to the Presidential Range, highest mountains in the northeast. To the west and north, hiking trails lead into the less rugged Crescent or Randolph Ranges of the northern White Mountains.

The 87-acre park has a large outdoor pool (known for its cold water), a small beach, and a bathhouse. There are separate picnic areas for families and organized groups. Trout fishing is excellent in many nearby streams. The campground is equipped with 42 tent sites, and is a popular base location for hiking trips into wilderness areas.

The main season runs from late June to Labor Day, with weekend camping permitted from mid-May on. Fees are charged for camping, and for day use during the main season.

6 MOUNT WASHINGTON STATE PARK

Sargent's Purchase

Nearest highway approaches are U.S. Route 302, north of Crawford Notch, and N.H. Route 16 at Pinkham Notch.

Mount Washington State Park, 6,288 feet above sea level, clings to the windy, rocky top of the highest peak in the northeastern United States. The park's 52 acres encircle the treeless summit of Mount Washington, completely surrounded by the White Mountain National Forest

On the rare clear days the view from the summit is unsurpassed. The world is spread out below. Nearby are Mounts Jefferson, Adams, and Madison, other peaks of the Presidential Range. Further away in all directions a rolling sea of mountain and forest marches off to the horizon. Far below, tiny cars snake their way along winding roads.

Mount Washington has been a place of awe and majesty since the days of the Indians. The first white man to climb the mountain was Darby Field in 1642. In 1784 a party of "gentlemen," including historian Reverend Jeremy Belknap, reached the summit. Belknap's group estimated the mountain's altitude at 10,000 feet. They named the peak to honor the hero of the Revolution, General George Washington, who became President five years later.

As population grew and travel increased, the mountain became a popular attraction. In 1853 the Tip Top House was constructed at the summit. Travel surged after the world's first carriage road opened in 1861 on the east side of the mountain, curving sinuously eight miles to the summit. Today visitors can drive their own cars up the carriage road, or ride in specially-equipped chauffeured vans. The world's first cog railway began operations in 1869, and coal-burning steam locomotives, loaded with

The summit of Mt. Washington, Dick Smith photograph.

tourists, still puff their way up the steep grades from Marshfield to the summit.

But Mount Washington is far more than a tourist attraction. It is a unique natural and scientific resource. The bare metamorphic rocks have been scoured by the glaciers. Farther down the mountain these same glaciers created Huntington and Tuckerman ravines, steep-sided cirques with bare slopes and sheer cliffs.

The summit plant life is like that of no other place in New England, a sparse growth of lichens and small shrubs, with rare colorful wildflowers blooming for a few brief weeks each spring. Similar to the flora of Labrador, many of the plants probably have existed on top of the mountain since the retreat of the glaciers.

The weather on Mount Washington has been called the worst in the world. Its climate, considerably more severe than the rest of New Hampshire, resembles parts of arctic Canada. Clear sunny days are rare. Snow has been recorded in every month of the year. Enough snow lingers in Tuckerman Ravine until late May or June to attract skiers for the last run of the season. The weather is known for its rapid changes. In the space of a few minutes, a rare warm, spring-like day can turn into a winter blizzard, with plummeting temperatures and rising wind.

Indeed, it is the wind that has made Mount Washington a meteorological wonder. The Mount Washington Observatory, a non-profit private organization, has been studying Mount Washington's climate for decades. The jet stream in the upper atmosphere blows eastward across the continent, often attaining speeds in excess of 100 miles per hour. As the stream crosses the Green Mountains of Vermont, it makes a slight downward dip. Directly in its path is Mount Washington. One result is the highest wind velocity known on land, 231 miles per hour. This record, noted by the Observatory in 1934, still stands today, and gale force winds are a frequent occurrence.

In summer mountain climbers scramble over the rocky slopes. After winter claims the mountain, the climbers may return for snow and ice climbing, especially in Huntington Ravine. The mountain has also attracted earth scientists, botanists, and even the military, which used the summit to study adaptations of men and equipment to severe weather.

The summit was acquired through bequest in 1951 by Dartmouth College, and sold to the state for a modest sum in 1964. For several years, the state, hampered by lack of funds, could do little to improve facilities.

Finally in 1980 the Sherman Adams Building was opened. Named in honor of the former governor, United States Senator, and aide to President Eisenhower, this two-story building is firmly anchored into bedrock. The carriage road and the cog railway both terminate just outside.

For visitors there is a gift shop, cafeteria, post office, information desk, and rest room facilities. All are accessible by the handicapped. Hikers have a special area reserved for them. The Mount Washington Observatory is housed in a separate wing. The building's flat roof has reinforced railings and walkways along its entire 240-foot length, providing visitors with safe unobstructed views in all directions. There are no overnight accommodations. The building's rugged construction was successfully tested a few weeks after it opened when 140-mile winds buffeted the structure.

Although most visitors reach the summit by cog railway or carriage road, the mountain attracts thousands of hikers each year. Numerous trails lead upward from the national forest on all sides of the mountain. Whatever the trail, the climb is long, steep, and arduous, and usually not for novices. Rapid changes in weather have claimed the lives of many unprepared hikers, even in summer. Check locally before attempting to climb Mount Washington.

The Sherman Adams visitor center is open from Memorial Day to Columbus Day. There is no charge for using the building, but fees are charged by the privately-owned cog railway and carriage road.

7 FOREST LAKE STATE BEACH

Dalton

On a local road off N.H. Route 116, 10 miles east of Littleton

In the foothills of the White Mountains, near the Connecticut River and the Vermont border, lies scenic Forest Lake. A small 50-acre area, it is one of the 10 original state parks created in 1935.

Along the lake is a 200-foot sandy beach, one of the northernmost bathing beaches in the state parks. A bathhouse is adjacent to the beach. The water remains cool well into the summer. Picnic sites, many in shaded birch groves, overlook the lake with the peaks of the White Mountains in the background.

The park is open weekends beginning Memorial Day, and daily from late-June through Labor Day. Following renovations in 1982, all facilities are accessible to handicapped individuals. A fee is charged.

Forest Lake State Beach, Douglas Armsden photograph.

8 WEEKS STATE HISTORIC SITE
Lancaster

Off U.S. Route 3, 2 miles south of Lancaster

Weeks State Historic Site on top of Mount Prospect was the summer home of John Wingate Weeks. As a congressman from Massachusetts, Weeks introduced legislation to establish the White Mountain National Forest and all national forests in the eastern United States.

Weeks was born in Lancaster in 1860. After attending the U.S. Naval Academy in Annapolis, Maryland, he moved to Massachusetts where he was elected to Congress. His New Hampshire background instilled in him a lifelong love of wilderness. As a congressman, he worked hard to establish federal

wilderness preserves. The so-called Weeks Bill, which led to the creation of the country-wide United States Forest system, became law in 1911. Weeks later was elected senator from Massachusetts, and he served as Secretary of War under Presidents Harding and Coolidge.

The site was once part of Week's larger Mount Prospect estate. Today it is an easy drive up a winding paved road through forested slopes to a large fieldstone and stucco mansion. A trophy room and mementos of Week's life are on exhibit. There are majestic views of the Presidential Range of the White

*Weeks Historic Site,
Don Sieburg photograph.*

Mountain National Forest, so beloved by Weeks, plus more distant views of the upper Connecticut River Valley and mountains in Maine and Vermont. Although the house is almost at the summit of the 2,058-foot peak, a stone observation tower provides an even better view. Several picnic sites are available. In springtime, wildflowers bloom in profusion on the slopes.

Originally known as Mount Prospect State Park, the land and buildings were a memorial gift to the people of New Hampshire by the senator's children, Sinclair Weeks and Katherine Weeks Davidge. The season runs daily from late June to Labor Day, and weekends through the end of September, weather permitting. The Weeks State Park Association assists the Division of Parks in maintaining this site. A fee is charged.

9 ANDROSCOGGIN WAYSIDE PARK
Errol

On N.H. Route 16, south of Errol

This one-acre wayside park lies within the scenic "Thirteen Mile Woods," a protected roadside and riverside zone along the Androscoggin River. The picturesque river was once a watery highway for the timber industry to transport their logs from forest to market. The log drives have been stopped, and the Androscoggin is once again a sparkling clear stream.

The many rapids, once the motive power for the logs, now make the river a favorite for canoeists. The park lies on a bluff overlooking a bend in the river. There are no fees.

10 NANSEN WAYSIDE PARK
Milan

On N.H. Route 16, 4 miles north of Berlin

The 170-foot steel tower of the state-owned Nansen Ski Jump looms over this wayside park along the banks of the Androscoggin River. A boat launching ramp provides access to the scenery and fish of the river. There are several picnic sites. No fee.

Crawford Notch, Guy Shorey photograph.

FRANCONIA NOTCH– CRAWFORD NOTCH REGION

11 CRAWFORD NOTCH STATE PARK

Harts Location

Along U.S. Route 302, 12 miles north of Bartlett

Crawford Notch snakes for six miles through some of the most rugged terrain in the White Mountains. Carved out by glacial ice, its U-shaped valley is flanked on both sides by tall mountains, topped by Mount Washington, highest peak in the northeast, less than ten miles away. In this narrow mountain pass, bare rock prominences rise up 2,000 to 3,000 feet on either side.

Timothy Nash, a hunter, discovered the head of the notch in 1771, but it probably was explored earlier by white men. A few years later Abel Crawford, who gave the notch his name, built a house there and supported himself through hunting, farming, and trapping. As travel increased the Crawford family began to provide for the needs of the visitors. In 1819 Abel and his son Ethan built a path to the summit of Mount Washington to accommodate the public.

Samuel Willey Jr. moved his family to the notch in 1824 and built the Willey house to service the increasing number of wagons traveling between settlements north of the mountains and markets on the seacoast. In August, 1826, a violent storm swept through the mountains, followed by severe floods. A few nights later water-soaked debris, lubricated and loosened by the rain, tore free from the side of the mountain. An avalanche roared down what is now Mount Willey, sweeping away everything in its path. When rescuers penetrated to the debris-strewn valley a few days later, they were surprised to find the Willey house undamaged but surrounded by boulders, trees, and tons of dirt on all sides. Nobody was in the house except a howling, hungry dog. Apparently the entire family had gone outside in an attempt to escape the avalanche only to run into its unstoppable force.

Seven people were killed in the disaster: Mr. and Mrs. Willey, their five children, and two hired men. Three of the bodies were never found. A plaque now marks the location of the house, and scars of the slide can still be seen on the mountain slopes above.

Driving through the notch today reveals mountainous grandeur at every bend. Two waterfalls — the Flume and the Silver Cascades — are visible from the highway.

The Appalachian Trail crosses near the center of the park. This, and other trails, lead into the surrounding White Mountain National Forest. A variety of hikes are available, ranging from short jaunts to week-long backpacking trips. A mile and a quarter walk leads to Arethusa Falls, one of the tallest waterfalls in the state. A self-guided nature trail leads through the woods just over the bridge across from the main park office. Below the bridge large trout lurk in the pool. There is no fishing permitted here but the pond above the bridge is stocked for children's fishing.

Other activities include fishing in the many mountain streams, and taking photographs. Several picnic sites are scattered about. Dry River Campground, three miles from the Willey House Memorial, provides 30 tent sites.

Additional campsites are found within the White Mountain National Forest. In summer you can buy articles made by blind New Hampshire artisans and craftsmen at the New Hampshire-Made Products cabin.

The park was established as the result of a hotel which was having financial difficulties. In 1909, the resort hotel Crawford House could not make its mortgage payments. Because the mortgage was secured by timber, the bank threatened to collect back payments in virgin spruce. Under pressure from the Society for the Protection of New Hampshire Forest, and aided by the Appalachian Mountain Club, the state appropriated funds in 1911 to acquire the notch. The virgin spruce still stands today.

The road through the notch is open all year. A fee is charged for use of the campground, open from mid-May through mid-October.

(above) The historic Willey House, Crawford Notch State Park. (below) A view of Mt. Willey, Crawford Notch, Dick Smith photograph.

12 FRANCONIA NOTCH STATE PARK

Franconia and Lincoln

On U.S. Route 3

Franconia Notch State Park lies in a deep valley surrounded by soaring peaks of the White Mountain National Forest. The park, which extends along U.S. Route 3 for eight miles, has been a year-round vacation and recreation area for generations. Popular activities include sightseeing, hiking, swimming, picnicking, camping, and skiing in a setting of spectacular beauty. It is New Hampshire's best known park, and includes the world-famous Old Man of the Mountain.

The present landscape received its final sculpting through the action of glacial ice several thousand years ago. The glaciers scraped bare the granite rocks, removing soil and weathered rock. As the ice melted, the valleys were partially filled with glacial debris, and the huge volume of meltwater scoured out today's lake beds, potholes, and basins.

The park is almost entirely surrounded by the White Mountain National Forest. Extending throughout the park is a network of hiking trails reaching to all parts of the White Mountains. The Appalachian Trail, which runs from Maine to Georgia, traverses the park near the Whitehouse Bridge.

The Cannon Tram II and Cannon Mountain are near the northern end of the park. The original aerial tramway, the first in the United States, began operations on Cannon Mountain in 1938, and helped the facility build into one of the country's leading ski resorts. A new system more than a mile long, Cannon Tram II, was completed in 1980.

Each car, holding 80 people and equipped with wheelchair safety belts, rises more than 2,000 feet vertically to the 4,180-foot summit of Cannon Mountain. As the traveler ascends during the 6-minute trip, the panorama of the White Mountains unfolds.

At the summit, walking trails lead to a variety of view points. The vegetation is restricted to mosses, scrub spruce trees, and springtime alpine flowers. A snack bar, rest rooms, and souvenir shop are available at both the base and the summit. Cannon Tram II operates from Memorial Day through mid-October for the non-skiers.

Cannon Tram II, Franconia Notch State Park, Dick Hamilton photograph.

When winter arrives skiers replace sightseers on the tram, and usually the car makes the downward trip empty. Spiderwebbing Cannon Mountain are 30 miles of ski trails and slopes, for all classes of skiers from novice to expert. A triple chair lift, two double chair lifts, and two T-bars augment the tram. Beginners have their own pony lift. A ski school, ski shop, and rental and repair facilities are on the premises. Snowmaking services most of the mountain, from the summit to the base, so that the ski season usually starts in December and lasts until April.

Many handicapped people also enjoy skiing at Cannon Mountain, with the help of the New England Handicapped Sportsmen's Association, a satellite of the major handicapped ski program at Mount Sunapee. As these individuals increase their skill in skiing, many also gain feelings of competence and confidence in other areas of life.

The Old Man of the Mountain, just south of Cannon Mountain, has long been the unofficial symbol of New Hampshire. Discovered in 1805, it was immortalized by Nathaniel Hawthorne in his classic short story, "The Great Stone Face." Also known as the Profile, the phenomenon is formed by five separate rock ledges 1,200 feet above Profile Lake. When viewed from the right spot it bears a striking likeness to the left side of a man's face. To slow erosion and deterioration, the five face-making ledges which measure about 40 feet from chin to forehead have been securely bolted and cemented to the mountainside.

The Flume is an 800-foot-long rock gorge at the south end of the park that visitors traverse on a reinforced boardwalk. The walls of this chasm, 12 to 20 feet apart, rise to a height of 60 to 70

The Old Man of the Mountain, Franconia Notch State Park, Moosilauke Studio photograph.

feet, while down below a rushing stream tumbles over boulders. The Flume began millions of years ago when a crack in the Conway granite filled with basalt, forming what geologists call a dike. When the mass was uplifted and exposed to the erosive power of water and ice, the less-resistant basalt wore away faster than the enclosing granite, leaving the present gorge.

The moist walls of the Flume support luxuriant growths of ferns and mosses. The Flume was discovered in 1808 by 93-year-old Aunt Jesse Guernsey who was looking for a good place to catch trout.

Nearby is Liberty Gorge and Cascades, the Sentinel Pine Bridge, and the Pool, a 40-foot deep clear pristine pothole surrounded by 130-foot cliffs.

A complete walking tour of the Flume and nearby features is about two miles. Round-trip shuttle bus service between the parking lot and the Flume reduces the walk to about 0.6 mile. The new George Gilman Visitor Center provides information and slide shows of nearby features. Souvenirs, restrooms, and snacks are available. The attraction is open from Memorial Day weekend to mid-October.

Echo Lake, just north of the tram, has 28 acres of glistening water with Artist's Bluff Overlook in the background. The lake, popular for swimming, boating, and fishing, has a sandy beach, bathhouse, and picnic sites.

Lafayette Campground near the center of the park is a family camping area with 98 tent sites, a recreation building, and showers. The camping season runs from late May to mid-October. The Appalachian Mountain Club maintains several huts for campers in the back country.

The Flume, George Sylvester photograph.

The Basin, between Lafayette Campground and the Flume, is a glacial pothole 20 feet in diameter at the foot of a small waterfall. It has been scoured smooth by water, sand, and stone.

There is a charge summer and winter to ride the aerial tram, and to purchase ski lift tickets. Skiers have a choice of lift packages, including individual rides, all day tickets, and season tickets. Admission is charged to visit the Flume, and there is a charge for camping.

26

Preserving the park has required continual vigilance. It was privately owned in 1923 when the Profile House, a leading resort hotel, burned to the ground. Lumber companies eyeing the virgin spruce were eager to snap up the 6,000 acres owned by the hotel. The Society for the Protection of New Hampshire Forests asked the owners if they would wait until the Society came up with the purchase money. The owners agreed, even though the Society had far less than the $400,000 asking price.

The New Hampshire legislature appropriated $200,000 for the notch in 1925, but left it up to the Society to raise the rest. A major fund raising campaign was launched. More than 15,000 contributors participated, many of them school children giving nickels or dimes; and in 1928 the notch was purchased.

The Society had planned to turn the notch over to the state. But the hotel companies no longer conducted tours through the Flume, and the state, which did not then have a parks department, was unwilling to accept it. So for 20 years, until 1948, the Society for the Protection of New Hampshire Forests led the visitors on tours through the granite sluiceway.

In recent years the park has faced threats equally as serious as the axes and saws of the lumber companies. Just outside the park, both north and south, lie the four lanes of Interstate 93, the main corridor through the heart of New Hampshire. Winding eight miles through the park is the last uncompleted stretch of interstate, the two lanes of U.S. 3. A four-lane highway built to interstate specifications through the narrow notch would irreparably alter many wilderness aspects of the park.

Once again compromise has saved

Sentinel Pine Bridge at the Flume, Franconia Notch State Park, George Sylvester photograph.

the notch. Outside the park, the road will be built to interstate standards, a divided four-lane highway. Within park boundaries, the road will be a divided two-lane parkway, with passing lanes on the hills. A bicycle path will meander through the woods nearby, separated from the roadway. This road will be one of only two locations in the country where an interstate highway has been built to less than four-lane interstate standards.

As the road is developed, many facilities will be enhanced and improved, and visitation patterns will change. Stop at the Gilman Visitor Center at the Flume for the latest information, or, turn your AM radio dial to 1610 for park and highway advisory messages while traveling through the notch.

27

Eisenhower Wayside Park, George Sylvester photograph.

13 EISENHOWER MEMORIAL WAYSIDE PARK

Carroll

On the east side of U.S. Route 302, 2 miles north of Crawford Notch State Park

This 7-acre memorial site, established in 1979 as a gift from the Bretton Woods Corporation, honors the late President Dwight D. Eisenhower. A short walk leads visitors to a view of the high peaks of the Presidential Range in the White Mountain National Forest. One of those peaks, formerly Mt. Pleasant, was renamed Mt. Eisenhower as part of this memorial.

There are no facilities and no fees.

14 WHITE MOUNTAIN NATIONAL FOREST

White Mountain National Forest in northern New Hampshire is the largest tract of public land in New England. Managed by the United States Forest Service, it covers about 750,000 acres, including 45,000 acres in Maine. It includes most of New England's highest peaks, and features more than 20 campgrounds and many picnic sites. There are 1,200 miles of hiking trails, 45 lakes and ponds, and 650 miles of fishable streams.

New Hampshire state parks are intertwined with the White Mountain National Forest. Some of the finest state parks—Franconia Notch, Mount Washington, Crawford Notch, Echo Lake— are entirely surrounded by the White Mountain National Forest; other parks — Moose Brook, Milan Hill — lie just outside the Forest boundaries.

First explored by Europeans in the 1600s, the region was permanently settled following the French and Indian War (1763) when the threat of Indian attack ended. As word of the beauty of the mountains spread, travel increased, and many of the original farmer settlers became innkeepers and hosts. By the 1850s, thousands were visiting the area. The Crawford Path to the top of Mt. Washington was built in 1819, and is still in use today.

Then came the railroads. Grand hotels, summer playgrounds for the urban east, sprang up. The railroads hauled lumber south to market and the logging industry flourished. Soon large areas were ravaged, cut bare and burned, to feed the growing demand for wood.

The logging industry, which almost ruined the mountains, ended up saving them. Pressure from conservation groups and concerned individuals led Congress to pass the Weeks Act in 1911 for the purchase of forest lands. Large sections of the White Mountains were acquired immediately.

The scarred landscape healed. Roads were upgraded as auto touring replaced railroad travel, and campgrounds were built.

Although the forest is managed for multiple use, auto touring remains the most popular activity today. The main routes through the forest are U.S. 3/I-93, which passes through Franconia Notch State Park; U.S. 302 through Crawford Notch State Park; and N.H. Route 16. Mount Washington State Park, sur-

Madison Hut with Mt. Adams at right and Mt. Washington in the background. White Mountain National Forest, Dick Smith photograph.

rounded by the forest, is accessible from U.S. 302 (cog railway), N.H. Route 16 (auto toll road) and by numerous trails. The northern section of the forest is adjacent to N.H. Routes 16 and 110, close to Milan Hill and Moose Brook State Parks. Activities in those parks are described elsewhere. There are numerous motels, restaurants, and other tourist facilities scattered throughout the region.

The 1,200 miles of hiking trails begin from major roads at over 200 locations. There are trails for all experience levels, from half-hour strollers to expert mountain climbers and backpackers. The Appalachian Trail, linking Georgia and Maine, crosses many major peaks and roads.

Camping and picnicking are also popular activities. Camping opportunities range from fully equipped campgrounds to secluded sites. Some remain open all winter. Daily fees are charged.

In autumn, the valleys and mountainsides turn to shades of red, gold, and yellow as tourist travel peaks. Advance reservations are recommended at this time, if you plan to stay overnight.

The Kancamagus Highway is a 34-mile scenic highway between Lincoln and Conway in the national forest. The drive passes through narrow stream gorges and breathtaking mountain overlooks. Several picnic sites and campgrounds lie along the route. Many trails, long and short, start at the highway.

Swimming is permitted in many of the streams and rivers. Lower Falls is one of the most popular spots.

Sabbaday Falls is reached by a 5-minute walk along the graded Sabbaday Brook Trail. There are self-guided trails in several places. There are two wilder-

Rocky Gorge, Kancamagus Highway, Douglas Armsden photograph.

ness areas within the White Mountain National Forest: Great Gulf Wilderness and the Presidential Range-Dry River Wilderness. No motorized vehicles are allowed.

Tuckerman Ravine on the east slopes of Mt. Washington is world famous for its spectacular scenery, deep snow, and mountaineering challenges. It can be reached only by an arduous hike, and should be attempted only by those in good physical condition.

In winter, snowshoeing, cross-country skiing, snowmobiling, and winter camping and hiking are popular. Huntington Ravine is known for its technical ice climbing. Alpine skiing is located at Cannon Mountain in Franconia Notch State Park, and at several private areas within the national forest.

For further information, contact the Forest Supervisor, P.O. Box 638, Laconia, NH 03247. National forest ranger stations are maintained in Bethlehem, Gorham, Plymouth, and Conway, New Hampshire, and Bethel, Maine.

Mt. Sunapee State Park.

SUNAPEE–PILLSBURY REGION

15 MOUNT SUNAPEE STATE PARK

Newbury

On N.H. Route 103, 3 miles west of Newbury

Mount Sunapee has long been known as a major ski resort. But the park is also a year-round recreation center. As seasons change, the park features hiking, skiing, crafts exhibits, picnics, and other activities. Nearby Sunapee State Beach provides swimming and beach activities.

The park's genesis was in 1910 as logging operations crept toward the summit of 2,720-foot Mount Sunapee. Soon the virgin forest was gone, except for one 256-acre tract along the crest of the mountain. Included in the virgin area was Lake Solitude, a glacial lake. Local citizens appealed to the Society for the Protection of New Hampshire Forests for help. A year later the Society had raised $8,000, enough to purchase more than 600 acres of mountain top. As additional funds became available over the years, the holdings were increased. The reservation was managed by the Society until 1948 when the state purchased it. The present park has over 2,700 acres.

Aerial lifts are in operation year round at the park. Both summer and winter the main chair lift whisks riders to the summit in 13 minutes. Riders gain 1,500 feet in elevation over the 6,800-foot trip.

On top is a lodge with observation platforms and a cafeteria. Far below can be seen sparkling Sunapee Lake. On clear days there are distant views northeast to New Hampshire's White Mountains, and west to Mount Ascutney and the Green Mountains of Vermont. A mile-long hiking trail leads to Lake Soli-

League of New Hampshire Craftsmen Fair, Mt. Sunapee State Park, David MacEachran photograph.

tude, still surrounded by virgin forest.

Mount Sunapee is the northern terminal of the Monadnock-Sunapee Greenway, a 51-mile hiking trail between these parks. A recreation corridor links Mount Sunapee with Pillsbury State Park.

At the base is a larger cafeteria, souvenir shop, and sun terrace. There are picnic sites, and an exhibition trout pool. An auditorium is available for group outings and displays.

Each summer the League of New Hampshire Craftsmen annual fair attracts more than 100 exhibitors. The park is also host to the Mayfest and Oktoberfest, state-wide festivals for dis-

Pillsbury State Park, Bob Swenson photograph.

abled and elderly citizens. Other events include a gem and mineral show, concerts, a bike race, and others.

Snowmaking and grooming bring early skiing, usually by mid-December. Skiers schuss down a 180-acre network of 23 slopes and trails from novice to expert. There are five double chair lifts, and a free pony lift for beginners. A ski school, rental and repair shop, apparel shop, and nursery are on site. With favorable weather and continued snow making, the ski season may run to mid-April.

Hundreds of physically handicapped people have learned to ski with the aid of the New England Handicapped Sportsmen's Association. As these individuals increase their skiing skills, many also increase their feelings of competence and confidence in other areas of life.

In summer fees are charged for lift rides. In winter skiers have available a variety of lift rates, ranging from individual rides to family season tickets.

16 PILLSBURY STATE PARK

Washington

On N.H. Route 31, 3½ miles north of Washington

Visitors to Pillsbury are usually delighted to discover or return to this relatively undisturbed and little developed wilderness of woods, ponds, wetlands, and hills. Many would be surprised to learn that today's quiet picnic areas and campsites once buzzed with the activity of sawmills, residences, and even a schoolhouse.

Early settlers, mostly farmers, called the area Cherry Valley because of the numerous cherry trees. Lumbering came to the valley in the 1780s, attracted by the many ponds with their water power to run sawmills.

Despite abundant timber, the mills often had hard times. Fire was a constant danger. The roller coaster

33

economy of the young nation encouraged clear cutting and depletion of timber during boom times, followed by abandonment when the economy turned sour.

The first mill burned, was rebuilt, and then sold to John May (for whom the largest pond in the park is named) in the early 1800s. But May found it easier and more profitable to collect tolls from travelers along the Croydon Turnpike (now Route 31), and to entice the weary visitors to tarry a while at his inn and tavern. Business was so good that he deliberately burned down the mill so he could concentrate on his other interests. May left about 1834 to run a larger inn in the then booming town of Washington Center.

Other mills followed: Butterfield, David Gove's, the P.C. Cheney Company, and more. All had similar histories of a few successful years followed by fire or economic disaster.

The last mill owner, Albert E. Pillsbury, was one of the nine founders of the Society for the Protection of New Hampshire Forests. In 1905 he bought 2,400 acres of cut-over land in Cherry Valley. But the mills stopped operating in 1915 from increased public concern about clear cutting and pond and stream pollution from sawdust and mill refuse. Pillsbury, a man of diverse interests, found he did not have enough time to manage his land, and in 1920 he deeded the property to the public "... as a public forest reservation..."

For the next three decades the area was managed by the state Forestry Commission. In 1935 it was turned over to the Parks Department. In the 1930s, the Civilian Conservation Commission restored or rebuilt several dams. An attempt was made to introduce elk from the Rocky Mountains to the park, when 12 were released in 1933. The last one was seen in 1955, although there are still occasional reports of elk being sighted on back trails. The last of the old buildings was removed in 1959, so there are no visible reminders today of the era of the lumber mills, except for the old dams.

Pillsbury State Park today is a near wilderness of more than 5,000 acres. Although the virgin trees are gone, the forest has reclaimed the land. Ponds once choked with sawdust again harbor wild ducks; and the cry of the loon can once more be heard.

Hiking is one of the most popular activities, with more than 20 miles of trails winding through the park. The park is a key link in the Monadnock-Sunapee Greenway, a 51-mile trail between these two parks. In 1975 the northern link, from Pillsbury to Sunapee, was completed when the state purchased a corridor of land 600 feet to a half-mile wide connecting the two.

Camping is restricted to 20 primitive sites on the shore of May Pond. Fishing is permitted in all seven of the park's ponds, and many are stocked yearly. Boats can be launched by the campsites. There are numerous picnic sites.

The park is open weekends starting Memorial Day, and daily from mid-June through Labor Day. Fees are charged for day use and for camping.

Sunapee State Beach, Bill Finney photograph.

17 SUNAPEE STATE BEACH

Newbury

On N.H. Route 103, 3 miles west of Newbury

Sunapee State Beach provides superb swimming in sparkling Sunapee Lake. The beach, a 900-foot strip of smooth sand, lies across the road from the ski slopes of Mt. Sunapee State Park.

Facilities include a large parking area, bathhouse, refreshment stand, and boat launching site. Spring-fed Sunapee Lake is noted for its game fishing. Rental boats are available nearby outside the park.

Summer activities are often combined with events taking place at Mt. Sunapee State Park, including the League of New Hampshire Craftsmen annual fair, the Mayfest and the Octoberfest, and others. See Mt. Sunapee State Park for details.

The beach season starts weekends in mid-May. It runs daily from mid-June to Labor Day, and weekends to mid-October. A fee is charged.

18 SAINT-GAUDENS NATIONAL HISTORIC SITE

Cornish

Off N.H. Route 12A, north of Claremont

Nestled in the hills of Cornish is the classical Greek and Roman home, garden, and studio of the American sculptor, Augustus Saint-Gaudens (1848 – 1907). Now a national historic site, the property was Saint-Gaudens' summer residence for many years, and his permanent home from 1900 until his death.

Saint-Gaudens was the foremost sculptor in the United States. He set standards for public monuments that have not been surpassed today, with his works gracing most major eastern cities. Among his better known works are the Shaw Memorial, the bronze relief gracing the Boston Common; the famed Puritan in Springfield, Massachusetts; General Sherman, at the entrance to New York's Central Park; the Adams Memorial in Rock Creek Cemetery,

Saint Gaudens National Historic Site.

Washington, D.C.; and the seated Lincoln in Chicago.

More than 100 replicas and original pieces are on exhibit at the site. Well known replicas include the Adams and Shaw memorials, and the Puritan. Saint-Gaudens was also well known for his cameos and bas (low level) relief. Numismatists will remember him as the designer of the beautiful eagle and double eagle gold coins ($10 and $20 pieces) struck from 1907 to 1933.

Also on exhibit is Aspet, the sculptor's home, plus studios, gardens, and other buildings. Original furnishings have been retained, many of which reflect the sculptor's interest in the classical Greek and Roman periods. You may also visit the Temple, the final resting place of the sculptor and his family, with graceful columns of Vermont marble. Special summer exhibits and concerts are sponsored by the Saint-Gaudens Memorial.

A two-mile hiking trail leads through the wetlands and woodlands of the Blow-Me-Down Natural Area. Born in New York and a long-time resident of Paris, the sculptor found relaxation, refreshment, and renewal here. In these quiet woods Saint-Gaudens hiked and skied, or skated on the surface of Blow-Me-Down Pond.

The site is administered by the National Park Service. It is open from late May through early October, and a fee is charged.

Echo Lake and White Horse Ledge, Echo Lake State Park, Dick Smith photograph.

CENTRAL REGION

19 ECHO LAKE STATE PARK

Bartlett and Conway

On local road off N.H. 302, 2 miles west of North Conway

Pristine Echo Lake nestles in the shadow of White Horse Ledge, just outside the resort town of North Conway. At the lake is a bathhouse, swimming, and picnic tables. A mile-long auto road leads to the top of nearby 700-foot Cathedral Ledge. Both White Horse Ledge and Cathedral Ledge have gradual slopes up their western flanks, with sheer drops of bare rock, scraped clean by former glaciers, to the east. A scenic trail around the lake gives magnificent views of both ledges.

At the top the view faces eastward across the Saco River Valley to the White Mountains. Both ledges can also be reached by hiking trails. Experienced rock climbers ascend the naked rock face, and rappel down into the valley. Winter mountaineering techniques are practiced in season.

In 1943 commercial development was planned for the lake. The Society for the Protection of New Hampshire Forests joined with the state to raise funds to buy the property, thus protecting it.

The park is open weekends starting

Echo Lake State Park, Douglas Armsden photograph.

Memorial Day, and daily from late June to Labor Day. A fee is charged.

20 MOUNT CARDIGAN STATE PARK

Orange

Off U.S. Route 4 and N.H. Route 118, 4½ miles east of Canaan

For the non-hiker, this park is primarily a scenic picnic area, set among the pines and rocks. Mount Cardigan, 3,121 feet high, is the crowning feature.

The entrance road west of the mountain leads to a parking and picnic area. The West Ridge Trail, shortest and easiest route to the summit, is a 1.3 mile hike

38

mit, is a 1.3 mile hike (one-way) with numerous sweeping vistas along the way. Non-hikers or novices should be careful before attempting this, or any other, hike.

The main peak, capped by a fire tower, is sometimes called "Old Baldy" because of its bare rock ledges. There is an especially good view of Mount Sunapee and Vermont's Mount Ascutney. Numerous trails lead from the summit. The South Peak lies a half-mile away along a ridge trail. To the north is Firescrew, a subsidiary peak that received its name in 1855 when the corkscrew of forest fires surrounding it could be seen for miles.

A network of trails totaling more than 30 miles encircles the mountain. Although the approach from the picnic area is most popular, routes lead to the summit from all directions. Many hikers use the Appalachian Mountain Club lodge, just outside the park boundary on the east side of Mount Cardigan, as a jumping-off spot. The lodge is about 9 miles west of N.H. Route 3A at the south end of Newfound Lake in Alexandria.

The park season runs from mid-May to mid-October. There are no fees.

White Lake State Park, George Sylvester photograph.

21 WHITE LAKE STATE PARK

Tamworth

On N.H. Route 16, ½ mile north of West Ossipee

White Lake State Park is one of the state's most popular camping spots. It's easy to see why, with the excellent hiking, swimming, fishing, and boating available. The lake itself formed from melting glacial ice that was buried beneath glacial debris called till. As the ice melted, it left a depression which was filled with water to form the present lake.

The beach area, wide and sandy, has a bathhouse, shelter, and refreshment stand. A large camping area provides 173 tent sites, sanitary facilities, and a ballfield. The picnic grounds are shaded by tall pines. In 1985 a 72-acre stand of the park's tall pitch pines (*Pinus rigida*) were designated a National Natural Landmark.

Trout fishing is good in the cool lake, and boating is permitted. There are a few rental boats available. Hiking is a popular pastime, with one trail encircling the lake.

After the winter's snows cover the ground, many of the park's trails are open for snowmobiling, cross-country skiing, and snowshoeing.

Fees are charged for day use and camping during the main season from late May through mid-October.

22 ELLACOYA STATE BEACH
Gilford

Route 11, Gilford

Lake Winnipesaukee, New Hampshire's largest lake with 72 square miles of water, has been a vacation center for more than 200 years. Most of the lake shore is privately owned, although surrounding communities maintain several public beaches. However, Ellacoya is the only state-owned beach on the lake.

Developed for swimming and beach activities, Ellacoya is a 600-foot long clean sandy beach on the southwest shore of Lake Winnipesaukee. On the far side of the lake are hauntingly beautiful views of the Sandwich and Ossipee mountains. There is a refresh-

Ellacoya State Beach, George Sylvester photograph.

ment stand and bathhouse. All facilities are accessible for the handicapped.

When the park opened, it had no name. School children throughout the state participated in a contest to supply one. A young girl won when she suggested "Ellacoya," the name of a little-known Indian maiden.

The beach is open weekends starting Memorial Day, and daily from mid-June to Labor Day. A fee is charged.

23 WELLINGTON STATE BEACH

Bristol

Off N.H. Route 3A, 4 miles north of Bristol

Wellington State Beach lies on a broad peninsula at scenic Newfound Lake. The sandy, half-mile long beach slopes down very gradually offshore. This provides some of the best lake swimming in the state, and makes it especially suitable for young children. Mountain foothills rise abruptly from the far shore of the lake.

Scattered along the beach in secluded coves are numerous picnic sites, many located in pine groves. Extending along the beach is the Lakeside Trail. Other scenic walks lead to rocky shores away from the beach, with many scenic views of the distant hills.

There is no general camping, but Cliff Island and Belle Island just off shore can be reserved for overnight camping by children's groups. There is a bathhouse and a snack bar. Fishing is popular in the spring-fed lake, but boats must be rented outside the beach from nearby concessions.

The season begins on weekends starting Memorial Day, and daily from late June through Labor Day. A fee is charged.

24 WENTWORTH STATE BEACH

Wolfeboro

On N.H. Route 109, 5 miles east of Wolfeboro

Lake Wentworth has been a vacation retreat for more than 200 years. In 1763 Royal Governor John Wentworth built a summer home there to escape the pressures of Portsmouth, the colonial capital. Most visitors today arrive by car, not horse and carriage, and nearby Lake Winnipesaukee is the more popular attraction. But Lake Wentworth's outstanding beauty probably would be better known if it were not overshadowed by its larger neighbor.

Wentworth State Beach is one of the smallest in the state park system, a compact 17 acres, and the only park in the Wolfeboro area. Its main feature is a sandy bathing beach on Lake Wentworth. Boating and fishing are popular, and rental boats are available. There is a bathhouse, a shaded picnic area, and a playfield.

The park is open weekends starting Memorial Day, and daily from mid-June to Labor Day, and a fee is charged.

25 MADISON BOULDER NATURAL AREA

Madison

On side road off N.H. Route 113, east of Madison

The Madison Boulder is a huge granitic rock, three stories high and more than 80 feet long. Originally it was embedded in the ground, part of the bedrock, probably near the top of a nearby mountain.

As the glacial ice sheet slowly advanced southward over New Hampshire, it plucked the boulder from the underlying rock and carried it along. When the glacier melted, the boulder was left in its present position.

Because of its huge size—a length of 83 feet, a width of 23 feet, and a height of 40 feet—the boulder is recognized as one of the largest glacial erratics in the world, and has been designated as a National Natural Landmark.

The area is accessible from late spring to late fall. There are no facilities and no fees.

26 PLUMMER LEDGE NATURAL AREA

Wentworth

2½ miles south of Wentworth on the town road along the north side of the Baker River

Plummer Ledge preserves about 10 glacial potholes, varying in size from two feet to more than 10 feet across. They formed as the glaciers melted when large volumes of running water were released from the melting ice.

Since then the forest has grown in and around the potholes, obscuring some, and depositing earth and debris in all of them.

This three-acre site was acquired in 1940 as a gift from George Plummer. There are no fees and no facilities.

27 SCULPTURED ROCKS NATURAL AREA

Groton

Between N.H. Routes 3A and 118, two miles west of Groton

The melting glaciers released large amounts of water into the Cockermouth River as it flowed toward Newfound Lake. Sand, pebbles, and rock fragments were borne along by the rushing torrent. Over time, the water and debris eroded out a miniature canyon 30 feet deep, and carved out potholes, smooth walls, and other interesting shapes into the bedrock.

There are several picnic sites. The park is accessible from late spring through early fall. There is no fee.

28 BEDELL BRIDGE HISTORIC SITE

Haverhill

On N.H. Routes 10 and 25, Haverhill

Haverhill, New Hampshire, and Newbury, Vermont are separated by the Connecticut River. In colonial days there was a ferry crossing, operated by Moody Bedell of Haverhill. In 1805 Bedell built the first bridge connecting

*Sculptured Rocks Natural Area,
Bill Bardsley photograph.*

the towns. Later he was to serve as a general in the War of 1812.

But the Connecticut River isn't kind to bridges. Spring floods with high water, ice floes, tree limbs, and debris wiped out Bedell's bridge. Floods also destroyed the next three replacement bridges after that. In 1866 a new bridge, 396 feet long, was built. Of the latest Burr-truss construction, it was the second longest two-span covered bridge in the country.

For years it served as an important link between the two states, carrying foot traffic, stage coaches, a railroad, and then automobiles. Until 1916 it was a toll bridge.

Then the 1927 flood battered it. The 1936 flood rose five feet above the bridge floor. In 1958 the bridge was declared unsafe and closed to traffic. A few years later it was donated to the state for restoration and designated a state park. But in 1973, before restoration, floods again damaged it, this time so severely that it was scheduled to be torn down.

Fund raising efforts to save the bridge generated more than $250,000, including grants from the National Park Service and private industry. With the help of covered bridge experts, the structure was renovated and restored.

But the river isn't kind to bridges. In September, 1979, two months after dedication, severe wind and heavy rains pelted the countryside. For hours wind and rain bore down unceasingly on the wooden structure, with the vertical sides catching the full force of the wind. The bridge, like its predecessors, could not stand the onslaught. The unceasing wind lifted it off the pilings. Swept downstream, it was totally destroyed, as the unknowing, uncaring wind and water swept by.

So today there is no bridge at Bedell Bridge. There are picnic tables. There are lovely views of the usually placid Connecticut River, cooled by zephyr breezes. There is a canoe put-in and landing area, giving access to some of the finest paddling along the upper Connecticut.

And the park itself was reevaluated. With its star attraction now totally a part of history, it no longer qualified as a full fledged state park. Redesignated as Bedell Bridge Historic Site, it is still a lovely place to picnic or canoe. And the blue Connecticut River flows serenely past a few old pilings.

Endicott Rock Historic Site, George Sylvester photograph.

29 ENDICOTT ROCK HISTORIC SITE
Laconia

At the south end of Weirs Beach, off U.S. Route 3

In 1652 the Massachusetts Bay Colony was expanding rapidly. As the colony grew to the north, the General Court decreed that the northern boundary began at a point three miles north of "the northernmost part of the river Merimacke [and then] upon a straight line east and west to each sea."

Royal Governor John Endicott had no interest in expanding west to the Pacific Ocean, wherever that might be. But he certainly was interested in the Atlantic seaboard with its desirable land and rich fishing and shipping industries.

So Endicott commissioned a four-man survey party, led by Captain Simon Willard and Captain Edward Johnson, to locate and mark the colony's northern boundary. With two Indian guides, the party pushed northward up the course of the Merrimack River.

Eventually they reached the point where the Pemigewasset and the Winnipesaukee rivers merge to form the Merrimack, in present-day Franklin, New Hampshire. The Indians insisted the Winnipesaukee was the true Merrimack. The party turned eastward and northward, following the river until they emerged on the shores of a great lake bordered by mountains. The Indians called the place Aquadoctan, and the lake Winnipesaukee.

On a large boulder the survey party carved their initials, and the royal governor's name. In the eighteenth century an obstruction in the Winnipesaukee River raised the surface of the river and lake. This inundated the rock, submerging it until 1833 when a dam was constructed in the river.

In 1885, after more than 200 years of exposure to the elements, the boulder was raised several feet above the high water mark, set in concrete, and enclosed within a protective granite structure where it remains today.

Today Aquadoctan is known as the Weirs, and the large rock is called Endicott Rock. It has been referred to by historians as the "oldest public monument" in New England.

Endicott Rock is just south of the Weirs in the town of Laconia on the north bank of the Winnipesaukee River. It was acquired by the Department of Parks and Recreation by purchase from the city of Laconia in 1934.

30 GOVERNOR WENTWORTH HISTORIC SITE
Wolfeboro

N.H. Route 109, Wolfeboro

The Governor Wentworth Historic Site, the location of the former summer home of New Hampshire's last colonial governor, is an active archaeological area under development.

The estate was planned in 1765 as the summer plantation for Royal Governor John Wentworth. It was abandoned by the governor at the time of the Revolution when he fled the colony of New Hampshire. The house was destroyed by fire in 1820.

Known archaeological remains include cellar holes for the mansion and dairy, a carriage house foundation, several wells, and a dam and mill site. Foundations of almost a dozen other buildings are known to exist, but have not been located. These include a smoke house, ashes house, cabinetmaker's shop, carpenter's shop, blacksmith's shop, barns, and tenant houses.

The site is under study through the cooperative efforts of several state agencies, including the New Hampshire Division of Parks and Recreation, the New Hampshire Historical Society, and the state's Historic Preservation Office.

Actual excavation and project management is being conducted by the New Hampshire State Cooperative Regional Archaeology Program (NH SCRAP) of the New Hampshire State Historic Preservation Office. Student archaeologists can earn college credit for their experience through the Institute for New Hampshire Studies at Plymouth State College. Volunteers are also welcome.

The site can be visited during the summer months. There are no facilities for visitors.

Governor Wentworth Historic Site, Mildred Beach photograph.

45

Gunstock County Recreation Area, George Sylvester photograph.

31 GUNSTOCK RECREATION AREA
Gilford

On N.H. Route 11A, Gilford

The Gunstock Recreation Area is a 2,000 acre ski resort and campground owned by Belknap County.

Gunstock Mountain has been a major ski resort for more than 40 years. Today it has some 20 slopes and trails from novice to expert. It is serviced by six double chair lifts, a platter pull, three T-bars and two ski jumps. Top to bottom snowmaking covers more than 80% of the slopes. From the ski touring center, a network of cross-country trails weave for 25 kilometers through the woods and hills. With snowmaking, skiing usually begins in December and lasts until April.

Facilities include a nursery, ski school, ski and rental shop, cafeteria, and after-ski lounge.

Each February the annual winter carnival features snow sculptures, games, and sleigh rides. Spring skiing is usually at its peak in March for the Maple Sugar Festival when both skiers and non-skiers can enjoy sugar house tours, woodsmen events, and a country craft show.

The Gunstock campground, spread out over the area's 2,000 acres, provides more than 300 campsites. Campers can choose brookside sites, pine forest, or open fields. Facilities and activities include an olympic size swimming pool, nine-acre fishing pond with paddleboats, horseback riding, store, playground, and shower room. Special events include dances, a community garage sale, craft and woodsmen festival, and an annual Oktoberfest.

The campground is open from late May through Columbus Day weekend. There is a fee.

Mt. Monadnock, Tom Blake photograph.

SOUTHWEST REGION

Greenfield State Park, Bob Swenson photograph.

32 GREENFIELD STATE PARK

Greenfield

On N.H. Route 136, 1 mile west of Greenfield

Greenfield State Park, set among the hills and woods of southern New Hampshire on Otter Lake, attracts many visitors from Nashua, Portsmouth, Manchester, and Massachusetts. Its 252 campsites make it the largest campground in the state park system, and one of the most popular.

Day visitors have a large beach for swimming, and bathhouse facilities. Picnic grounds for families are nearby, with special areas for organized groups such as scouts.

Camping facilities include numerous restrooms, a separate camping area for groups, and a shower building. A 900-foot beach is reserved for campers.

For all visitors there is a refreshment stand, boat rentals, and a boat launching ramp. Boat speed is restricted on Otter Lake, but fishing is usually good. Trails through the woods lead to several small ponds visited by walkers in summer and snowmobilers in winter. There are trails for cross-country skiing.

The park is open all year. The summer season begins weekends on Memorial Day, and runs daily from late June to early October. There are fees for camping and for day use.

33 MILLER STATE PARK

Peterborough

On N.H. Route 101, 3 miles west of Peterborough

Miller State Park, on top of South Pack Monadnock Mountain, is the oldest park in New Hampshire. It was established in 1891 by donation to the state as a memorial to General James

Miller, hero of the battle of Lundy's Lane in the War of 1812. There were no state parks then, no national forests, and very little publicly owned land.

Today a paved road winds 1.3 miles from U.S. highway 101 to the open slabby summit of the 2,288-foot high peak. At the top are picnic tables, a lean-to shelter, and a fire tower. To the west is an impressive view of the distinctive profile of Mount Monadnock, 12 miles distant. Other peaks and hills of southern New Hampshire and adjacent Massachusetts can be seen. During the fall foliage season the hills are ablaze with red, yellow, and orange. On clear days the skyscrapers of Boston are visible on the horizon. There are several short walking trails around the summit area.

From the base parking lot the Wapack Trail to the west and the Blue Trail to the east both lead to the summit, making possible a loop hike with no retracing. From the summit, the Wapack Trail leads north to neighboring Wapack National Wildlife Refuge, capped by North Pack Monadnock Mountain. Tradition says that the mountains were named by the Indians, and that the word "pack" means "little." The name is apt, for there is no confusing these smaller peaks with their larger namesake.

Visitation can be heavy on summer weekends or during the fall foliage season. The scenic views from the cool summit — accessible by car — and the closeness to the heavily populated areas of New Hampshire and Massachusetts make this park a popular one.

The park is named for General James Miller, long-time resident of nearby Temple, New Hampshire. Miller fought in the battles of Chippewa, Niagara, Erie, and Lundy's Lane. Following the war, he served as the first territorial governor of Arkansas. Later he worked with the author Nathaniel Hawthorne who referred to Miller as "New England's most distinguished soldier" in his introduction to *The Scarlet Letter*.

The park is open weekends from Memorial Day, and open daily from late May to mid-October, weather permitting. A fee is charged.

Miller State Park, Eric Sanford photograph.

34 MONADNOCK STATE PARK

Jaffrey

Off N.H. Route 124, 4 miles north of Jaffrey

The isolated peak of the Grand Monadnock has been the most prominent feature of southwest New Hampshire from the time of the glaciers. Since the first ascent by Europeans in 1706, Monadnock has been visited by millions.

It was the Indians who named the mountain "Monadnock," which means "standing alone." Geologists now call any isolated mountain rising above an eroded plain a monadnock. The peak reaches a height of 3,165 feet, only 1,500 to 2,000 feet above the adjacent lowlands. But the top 300 to 500 feet is bare rock ledge, the result of fires set by early settlers to drive wolves away from their sheep. The wolves are found no more, but the resulting view is unrestricted in all directions.

Only 65 miles from Boston, Massachusetts, the mountain has been a popular vacation destination for over a century. The Halfway House resort — burned down for the last time in 1954 — attracted many notables. Henry David Thoreau visited Monadnock several times, but when he camped there in 1860 he found it too crowded, littered, and covered with graffiti for his tastes. Ralph Waldo Emerson wrote a poem about the mountain. Mark Twain spent several weeks there in 1906.

Mount Monadnock has been called the world's second most climbed mountain, exceeded only by Japan's sacred Mount Fujiyama. At one time there were some 80 trails to the summit. Today less than a dozen are maintained,

and scores of others have been reclaimed by the mountain.

The state park is a 900-acre preserve on the west side of the mountain. This accounts for only a fraction of the publicly owned lands on Mount Monadnock. The first public ownership of land occurred in 1884 when the town of Jaffrey acquired a parcel on the south side of the peak. The first state park lands were acquired in 1905.

The state park area is reached over the Poole Memorial Road, originally built in 1802. In the 1920s Joel Poole improved the road and presented it and the surrounding land to the state as a memorial to his son, Arthur Eugene Poole. Other donations soon followed. In 1915 the Society for the Protection of New Hampshire Forests purchased the summit and 600 acres from the heirs of the original owners who had acquired the land in 1746. Under terms of the colonial royal grant, title to the mountain top was held in common in undivided form to the descendants of the settlers who owned the valley farms. The Society had to trace down and secure deeds from 89 heirs of the original owners. Final settlement required a decision by the New Hampshire Supreme Court.

Additional lots were added later by gift or purchase, so that the Society now owns more than 3,600 acres. The Halfway House and road were purchased in 1945 by the Association to Protect Mount Monadnock.

Mount Monadnock.

The entire complex of state park, summit, and other public lands is managed by the Division of Parks under cooperative agreements.

During the depression years of the 1930s various government programs provided money and manpower to improve the park. Now it has a picnic area with scenic views, a shelter, and a snack bar. Visitation can be heavy on summer weekends.

The camping area, open all year, has 21 family tent areas plus seven youth group sites. Nearby Spooky Woods — a dense stand of large white pines—remains dim even on the brightest of days. Ski touring is popular in winter.

The Monadnock Eco-center, a joint endeavor of the Society for the Protection of New Hampshire Forests and the New Hampshire Division of Parks, has geological and historical exhibits. Naturalists conduct guided tours, present slide programs, answer visitor's questions, and provide information on hikes and trails. The building and exhibits are accessible to the handicapped. A half-mile self-guided nature walk starts outside the Eco-center.

Several trails to the summit also originate at the Eco-center. The shortest summit trips are about 2.3 miles (one way) and take 3½ to 4 hours for a round trip. Be sure you are physically prepared and have proper equipment. Remember that there are about 30 miles of maintained trails covering the mountain, and most of them do not lead back to the state park.

The view from the summit, free from fire towers and antennas, encompasses all the New England states and part of New York. When conditions are right you can see the Boston skyline. The sparse plant growth is limited to shrubs and stunted spruce growing among the strongly folded metamorphic rock. Glacial grooves and scratches indicate the direction of ice movement, and there are many erratics—boulders transported by the ice and stranded when it melted.

The peak is the southern terminal of the Monadnock-Sunapee Greenway, a 51-mile trail linking those two parks and also passing through Pillsbury State Park. The peak is also the northern terminal of the 160-mile Metacomet Trail which traverses Rhododendron State Park and then winds southward to the Hanging Hills of Meriden, Connecticut.

Monadnock State Park is open all year. Fees are charged in the summer months for both day use and camping.

35 ROLLINS STATE PARK
Warner

Off N.H. 103, 4 miles north of Warner

Mount Kearsarge, 2,937 feet high, is flanked by Rollins State Park on the south, and Winslow State Park on the north. In 1874 the Warner and Kearsarge Road Company completed a winding toll road 3½ miles up the southern slope of Mount Kearsarge. A paved road today, its many scenic turnouts and views lead to a parking area and picnic sites about a half-mile from the summit.

From there a walking trail meanders upward to the bare gneiss and schist rocks of the summit. A fire tower, radio beacon, and warden's cabin seem

Rollins State Park, Bill Finney photograph.

to cling to the glacially scoured rocks. On clear days peaks of the White Mountains, Mount Monadnock, and mountains of Vermont can be seen. The fire tower affords an even better view, and one that is out of the wind. In autumn migrating hawks are often sighted.

Not usually confused with hawks are the hang-gliders, who, like prehistoric pterodactyls, launch themselves toward the parking area far below.

Land for the park and highway was given to the state over a period of years by the Society for the Protection of New Hampshire Forests. Originally called Kearsarge State Reservation or Tollgate State Park, it was renamed in honor of the late Frank West Rollins, former New Hampshire governor and a founding member of the Society. The park is open weekends starting Memorial Day, and daily from early June through October. A fee is charged.

36 WINSLOW STATE PARK
Wilmot

Off N.H. Route 11, 3 miles south of Wilmot

From Wilmot a well marked paved road leads to Winslow State Park, one of two parks on Mount Kearsarge. The park is named in honor of John A. Winslow, a Union admiral during the Civil War. In 1864 Admiral Winslow, commander of the sloop *Kearsarge*, sank the Confederate gunboat *Alabama* during a decisive battle.

A year later a large resort hotel, the Winslow House, was built on Mount Kearsarge near the present parking area. The hotel was severely damaged by fire in 1867. Although it was rebuilt, it

proved unprofitable, and was abandoned several years later.

The auto road climbs to the 1,820-foot level of the 2,937-foot mountain. At road's end are picnic sites and comfort facilities, the cellar hole for the Winslow House, and a steep mile-long trail to the summit.

At the top, a 360-degree panorama stretches out. There is a fire tower and warden's cabin. When the wind is right, hang-gliders hurl themselves into space, and, with luck, land in the parking area far below.

Winslow is open weekends starting Memorial Day, and daily from early June through mid-October. A fee is charged.

37 WADLEIGH STATE BEACH
Sutton

On N.H. Route 114 in North Sutton

Wadleigh State Beach is primarily a fine place to swim and picnic. It lies on Kezar Lake on the outskirts of the picturesque village of North Sutton. The sandy beach slopes gradually into the water. The picnic area, shaded by large pines, has separate facilities for families and large groups. There is a bathhouse and a large playfield. Rental boats are available and fishing is popular. A refreshment stand is nearby.

The park was established in 1934 as a gift from the Society for the Protection of New Hampshire Forests and the townspeople of Sutton. The season runs weekends from Memorial Day, and daily from mid-June to Labor Day. A fee is charged.

38 CHESTERFIELD GORGE NATURAL AREA

Chesterfield

On N.H. Route 9, Chesterfield

One man's generosity has preserved Chesterfield Gorge, a small but scenic park adjacent to the highway. The gorge was created when a stream, following the sinuous folds of the metamorphic rock, wore away the softer rock layers. Small box-like canyons were formed as the water swirled and plunged down the folds of the rock. Today the beauty is enhanced by the roar of the rapids, the smell of the spray, and the serenity of the quiet pools surrounded by lush green woods.

George White, a Chesterfield farmer, bought the land in 1936 to keep encroaching loggers from clear-cutting it. For $1,000 he sold 15 acres of the gorge to the Society for the Protection of New Hampshire Forests. The Society then donated it to the state of New Hampshire.

The trail through the gorge is a walk of about a half-mile, and it crosses the stream several times. Numerous picnic tables are available. The park is open weekends from Memorial Day, and daily from late June to mid-October, weather permitting. A fee is charged on weekends and holidays.

39 PISGAH NATURAL AREA

Chesterfield, Hinsdale, Winchester

Off N.H. Route 63, 2 miles east of Chesterfield

The Pisgah area is an undeveloped 13,000-acre tree-covered wilderness. For those willing to follow old logging trails, it offers excellent hiking, hunting, cross-country skiing, and snowmobiling. It has a small stand of virgin white pine, missed by the loggers. The many ponds are a challenge and delight to the back country fisherman, and birders will find good sightings in the remote marshes and swamps. Visitors should be adequately prepared and equipped for a semi-wilderness experience.

There are several approaches to the park. The most visited region is reached by turning east off N.H. Route 63 at Chesterfield. The parking area, about two miles from town, is marked by a memorial to former United States Supreme Court Chief Justice (1941 – 1946) Harlan F. Stone, who was born nearby.

The southern and eastern portions of the park are generally low ridges with shallow valleys, often marshy, in between. To the northwest a series of ridges culminates in Mount Pisgah, about 1,300 feet high. In the Old Testament, Mount Pisgah is the gateway to the Promised Land, beyond the mountain. Perhaps the early settlers who farmed the fertile valleys (now overgrown) in the shadow of the mountain felt they had found the Promised Land.

Other than a parking lot and pit toilets, the park has no facilities. Overnight camping and campfires are not permitted. There are no fees.

40 RHODODENDRON NATURAL AREA

Fitzwilliam

Off N.H. Route 12, 2½ miles north of Fitzwilliam

Mid-July brings the blooming of more than 16 acres of *Rhododendron maximum*, this park's namesake and most dominant wildflower. The pink and white blossoms contrast delightfully with the green of the leaves before a backdrop of sheltering pines.

Other wildflowers are found in abundance from early spring until the chills of autumn. Apple blossom time in May brings jack-in-the-pulpit, trillium, bloodroot, and Dutchman's breeches. Mountain laurel appears in June, followed by pipsissewa, pink lady's slipper, and rhododendron. In late summer Indian pipe and aster bloom. When October comes the hillsides flame with color, followed soon by the quiet white mantle of winter.

Rhododendron and mountain laurel need acid soil for growth. They do best where evergreens and oaks drop their needles and leaves to provide deep acid humus. The park contains the largest grove of rhododendrons in the northeast. The flowers, designated a National Natural Landmark in 1982, are at their peak for about a week in mid-July, but the exact dates vary year to year.

The grove was almost destroyed in 1902 when logging operations threatened to annihilate the rhododendrons. To save the tract, botanist Mary Lee Ware purchased 300 acres including the grove and surrounding land, and conveyed the deed to the Appalachian Mountain Club. The club managed the old Captain Samuel Patch cottage as a

Rhododendron Natural Area,
Bill Finney photograph.

hostel for many years, and donated the entire tract to the state of New Hampshire in 1946.

Winter storms in 1977 blew down numerous trees and branches, crushing much of the grove. After the downed trees were removed, the Fitzwilliam Garden Club developed the present outstanding Wildflower Trail that winds for one mile through the heart of the grove.

Other trails lead through hills and woods, including a fine hemlock forest, to scenic views of Mount Monadnock, about eight miles away. The Metacomet Trail, a hiking trail stretching 160 miles from Monadnock to Meriden, Connecticut, passes through the park.

A picnic area is nestled in the pine-hemlock forest. The park is open all year, with the busiest season in the spring and summer months, particularly mid-July. The Friends of The Old Patch Place, Inc. assist the Division of Parks in maintaining the site. Fees may be charged on weekends and holidays.

Franklin Pierce Homestead Historic Site, Eric Sanford photograph.

41 FRANKLIN PIERCE HOMESTEAD HISTORIC SITE
Hillsborough

Located near the junction of N.H. Routes 9 and 31

The Franklin Pierce Homestead was the boyhood home of the 14th president of the United States. It was built in 1804, the year Franklin Pierce was born. The house, a white, hip-roofed twin chimney colonial, reveals the graciousness and affluent living of the 19th century.

Restored in 1965 to reflect conditions during Pierce's boyhood, the house has wide board floors, wainscoting, and other old features. It is complemented by period-type furnishings similar to those of Pierce's boyhood. A ballroom runs the entire length of the second floor. The house has been placed on the register of National Historic Landmarks. Tours are conducted by the Hillsborough Historical

President Franklin Pierce.

56

Society, which maintains the site under a lease arrangement with the Division of Parks.

Pierce attended local schools and graduated from Bowdoin College in Maine. Like his father, Benjamin Pierce, who was twice elected governor of New Hampshire, the younger man entered politics. A Democrat, he held several state offices, and he was both a United States Congressman and Senator. He resigned to practice law in Concord. In 1852 he was nominated as a compromise candidate for the Democratic Party, and elected by a nation split on the slavery issue.

During Pierce's incumbency Commodore M. C. Perry led the successful Japanese expedition, and the Gadsden Purchase from Mexico added lands north of the Rio Grande to the country. In the 1850s the country was torn by regional differences. Pierce's attempts to smooth over the differences, and his opposition to the impending Civil War, made him unpopular both north and south, and he was not nominated for a second term.

The home is open from late May to mid-October. A fee is charged.

42 ANNETT WAYSIDE PARK

Rindge

On N.H. Route 119, Rindge

This seven-acre site, adjacent to the Cathedral of the Pines National Shrine, has a choice of picnic tables in shaded woods or in the open. A small fee is charged on weekends and holidays.

The park is part of the 1,300 acre Annett State Forest, donated by Albert Annett, former Governor's Councillor and an industrialist from nearby Jaffrey, New Hampshire.

43 GARDNER MEMORIAL WAYSIDE PARK

Springfield and Wilmot

On N.H. Route 4A, 4 miles north of Wilmot Center

This park, opened in 1980, memorializes Walter C. Gardner III, whose father established Gile State Forest.

The memorial includes a picnic area, land adjacent to Butterfield Pond, and an old mill site. There is no fee.

44 HONEY BROOK WAYSIDE PARK

Lempster

Off N.H. Route 10, Lempster

This one-acre park provides a restful picnic spot among shaded pine trees. No fee.

45 WAPACK NATIONAL WILDLIFE REFUGE

Greenfield and Temple

Off N.H. 101 at Miller State Park, Peterborough

The first national wildlife refuge established in New Hampshire, Wapack is located on North Pack Monadnock Mountain, just northeast of Miller State Park.

A popular hawk migration area, Wapack National Wildlife Refuge provides nesting habitat for many migratory songbird species such as tree sparrows, wrens, and thrushes. Permanent residents include ruffed grouse, woodpeckers, deer, mink, porcupine, fox, bobcat, and other mammals. About 90 percent of the refuge's 1,672 acres are timbered, but it also contains bog, swamp, bare rock ledge, and cliff.

Wildlife observation, photography, hiking, cross-country skiing, and snowshoeing are permitted. Hunting, trapping, camping, and fires are prohibited.

A three-mile segment of the Wapack Trail passes through the center of the refuge. The trail is accessible from the south from Miller State Park, Peterborough (both from the summit and the base), and from the north from Old Mountain Road, Greenfield.

The refuge is open all year for daytime use only. There are no fees. It is managed by the U.S. Fish and Wildlife Service through the Great Meadows National Wildlife Refuge, Sudbury, Massachusetts 01776.

Clough State Park, Virginia Sanford photograph.

SOUTHEAST REGION

Bear Brook State Park, Bill Finney photograph.

46 BEAR BROOK STATE PARK

.Allenstown

Off N.H. Route 28, 3 miles northeast of Hooksett

On summer weekends swimmers and picnickers from nearby Concord and Manchester swarm to Bear Brook's cool waters and shaded glens. This large park—over 9,000 heavily forested acres — has so many varied activities among its rolling hills that it is able to accommodate the thousands that flock to it.

The destination for many is the swimming beach and bathhouse on Catamount Pond, one of the park's six lakes. The picnic area adjacent to the beach has facilities for 1,500 visitors among tall pines. There is also a ballfield,

playground, and a large shelter. Rowboats can be rented to explore the shore line or just soak up the sun. Motors are not permitted, preserving the quiet and purity of the lake.

The campground and facilities on Beaver Pond are exclusively for campers, closed to day visitors. There are 81 tent sites, a swimming beach, and a play area with a ballfield. There is a separate youth group campground for scouts and similar organizations.

The National Park Service laid out the park as a Civilian Conservation Corps pilot project in the 1930s. You can still see many of the log buildings constructed by CCC workers. The park was leased to the state in 1941. Two years later the state was given title to the park. After World War II, the state continued to develop the park for multiple use.

The Bear Brook Nature Center, run cooperatively with the New Hampshire Audubon Society, is open to all visitors. Park naturalists schedule daily programs in summer, including walks, interpretive talks, evening slide shows, and movies. There are two self-guiding nature trails. The nature center houses a library and numerous exhibits, including the popular glass beehive.

Criss-crossing the park are more than 30 miles of hiking trails. Most of them lead away from the heavily utilized areas for those seeking solitude. Joggers are welcome to run along them, but they may prefer the physical fitness course with 20 stations. Archers can improve their skills on the 28-target course (rental equipment not available) to prepare them for the bow and arrow preseason deer hunting held here each fall.

Fishing is a popular pastime on many ponds and streams. Archery Pond is reserved for fly fishing. Two complete summer camps are used by organized groups, and are available for off-season rental.

After snow covers the woods, the hiking trails become the realm of the cross-country skiers and snowmobilers. To avoid possible conflict, miles of separately marked courses are laid out for these two groups.

The summer season runs from mid-May to mid-October, although some activities are available year-round. Fees are charged in season for both day use and camping.

47 CLOUGH STATE PARK
Weare

Between N.H. Routes 114 and 13, about 5 miles east of Weare

Floods were a seasonal hazard along the Piscatquog River until the United States Corps of Engineers established the Hopkinton-Everett Flood Control project, and built the earth-fill Everett Dam. This stabilized the river by creating 150-acre Everett Lake, now the site of Clough State Park.

The dam proved its worth in the spring of 1984 when record rainfall pushed the water level in Everett Lake to an all-time high. By summer, however, the 50-acre recreational park was ready for the heavy weekend crowds from nearby Concord and Manchester.

Facilities include a 900-foot sandy beach and two large bathhouses. Rental boats are available, or you can bring your own and launch it at the park's ramp. Motorized boats are not permitted. There is a large picnic grove and playground.

The park is open for day use only. The season runs weekends from Memorial Day, and daily from late June to Labor Day. A fee is charged.

Pawtuckaway State Park, Douglas Armsden photograph.

48 PAWTUCKAWAY STATE PARK
Nottingham

At Raymond, 3½ miles north of the junction of N.H. Routes 101 and 156

Located on beautiful 803-acre Lake Pawtuckaway in fast growing southeastern New Hampshire, Pawtuckaway State Park lies within a 45-minute drive of the population centers of Nashua, Concord, Manchester, Portsmouth, and Salem. Its 5,500 acres were developed in the mid 1960s for multiple use for both day visitors and campers.

The beach area, 900 feet long, has a large swimming dock and nearby bathhouse. There is a 25-acre wooded picnic ground for families, with a separate picnic site for scouts and other organized groups. The lake is stocked, and fishing is good. Rental boats are available and outboard motors are permitted. There is a refreshment stand, playfield, and shelter building.

Camping areas on Horse Island and Big Island (both accessible to autos via bridges) have a total of 170 tent sites, many directly on the water. There is a boat launching ramp, exclusively for campers, on Horse Island.

The park has an extensive oak-hickory forest, and a hemlock ravine. A nature trail leads past marsh, stream, and forest where you may see trees gnawed by beavers.

Away from the crowds, the Pawtuckaway Mountains form a group of three low lying ridges, erosional remnants of ancient volcanoes last active some 275 million years ago. Some of the rock types almost encircle the mountains, forming structures known as ring dikes.

Hiking trails to the mountains lead off from the main park area, or by car off New Hampshire Route 107 about 6 miles north of Raymond. The best views are from the fire tower atop South Peak, 908 feet high. On clear days it is possible to see north to Mount Washington and southeast to the Atlantic Ocean. The trail to North Peak, elevation 1,011 feet, passes several huge boulders 30 feet high. These gifts of the glaciers were transported by the ice and deposited here when it melted.

Snowmobiling, cross country skiing, and snowshoeing are popular in winter.

The main season extends from mid-May to mid-October. Fees are charged for day use and camping.

49 KINGSTON STATE BEACH

Kingston

Off N.H. Route 125 south of Kingston

Only 14 miles from the seacoast, Kingston State Park provides fresh water swimming on the north shore of Great Pond. The pond formed as the glaciers melted. A large, lingering mass of ice was buried beneath sand and gravel washed in from the main melting glacier. Years—perhaps centuries—later when the buried ice finally melted, the sand and gravel caved in, leaving a depression known as a kettle hole, surrounded by sandplain. Today Great Pond fills up the kettle hole.

Although this is one of the smallest parks, its 44 acres bustle with activity. There is a bathhouse, pleasant wooded picnic groves, and playing fields. Bird watchers will want to visit a small swamp where shore birds mingle with inland species. The park is open weekends starting Memorial Day, and daily from late June to Labor Day. A fee is charged.

50 SILVER LAKE STATE BEACH

Hollis

On N.H. Route 122, 1 mile north of Hollis

This swimming and picnic area attracts large crowds from nearby Nashua on summer weekends. Its main attraction is a 1,000 foot-long curved sandy beach at the north end of Silver Lake.

Much of the park consists of tall, shaded groves of pines. More than 100 picnic sites are scattered throughout the park's 80 hilly acres.

There is a bathhouse, a centrally located refreshment stand, and plenty of convenient parking. Close by on Silver Lake is Joy Farm, former summer home of the late poet, e. e. cummings.

The park is open weekends starting Memorial Day, and daily from mid-June to Labor Day. A fee is charged for parking and admission.

51 HANNAH DUSTON MEMORIAL HISTORIC SITE

Boscawen

Located just west of I-93, exit 17, 4 miles north of Concord

For years Hannah Duston has been singled out as an outstanding example of the heroism of the pioneer frontier woman. On March 15, 1697, Mrs. Duston, 39 years old and mother of 12 children, was captured by marauding Indians from her home in Haverhill Massachusetts. The Indians killed 27 persons during the raid, including the Duston's week-old daughter, and set fire to the town. Mrs. Duston's husband, Thomas, who was working in the fields during the raid, managed to escape with the couple's seven other living children.

The Indians also captured a neighbor, Mary Neff. During an earlier raid in Worcester, Massachusetts, they had taken 14-year old Samuel Leonardson captive. By canoe, the party of 12 Indians (including women and children) and three prisoners started up the Merrimack River through the wilderness for Canada.

During the night of March 30,1697, the party camped on a small island north of Concord in what is now the town of Boscawen, where the Contoocook River joins the Merrimack. As the Indians slept, Mrs. Duston and her companions stole their tomahawks and attacked their captors. Two Indians escaped, but they killed and scalped the remaining 10. They wrecked all but one of the canoes, and set off down river. Putting ashore at Dunstable, outside of Nashua, they continued on to Haverhill by foot.

In 1694 the Massachusetts colony (which claimed the Merrimack River

Hannah Duston Memorial Historic Site, George Sylvester photograph.

and surrounding territory in the New Hampshire colony) awarded a bounty of 50 British pounds for each Indian scalp. The bounty was reduced a year later, and then revoked completely in 1696. However, Thomas Duston, on behalf of his wife and her companions, presented the scalps and a petition for bounty to the Massachusetts governor and council in Boston. The petition was approved, and payment was voted on April 27, 1697 by the Massachusetts General Court. Mrs. Duston was awarded 25 pounds, and Mary Neff and Samuel Leonardson each received 12 pounds 10 shillings.

In 1874 a 35-foot high granite monument and statue of Hannah Duston was placed at the site of the escape in Boscawen. The monument and surrounding island, except for the railroad right of way, was deeded to the state. It shows Mrs. Duston, tomahawk in one hand and what looks like scalps in the other, peering out into the wilderness. Reputedly this was the first statue of a colonial woman to be erected in the United States.

The monument's centennial, celebrated at the island in 1974, was not without controversy. Indians and other groups objected to the monument (and the centennial celebration) claiming that the Duston party had slaughtered and scalped innocent women and children during their escape, and the entire matter glorified butchery and killing rather than heroism.

Now known as Duston Island, the monument is easily accessible from the well-marked parking area just off I-93. The monument is open all year, but the trail from the parking lot is not plowed. There are no fees.

52 ROBERT FROST FARM HISTORIC SITE
Derry

On N.H. 28, 2 miles south of Derry

"Good fences make good neighbors," said Napoleon Guay to his friend and neighbor Robert Frost. They were replacing the rocks on the wall knocked down by the winter's storms. Frost, who spent ten years at his Derry farm, was to remember and immortalize his neighbor's words.

The poet whose writings are the epitome of New England was born in San Francisco in 1874. After the death of his father from tuberculosis, his mother moved the family to Lawrence, Massachusetts, just south of the New Hampshire border.

Frost came to Derry in 1900 with his wife and former childhood sweetheart, Elinor, and their baby daughter Lesley. He was 25 years old. These were difficult days for him. His four-year old son had just died from cholera, and his mother was terminally ill with cancer. Frost himself expected to die soon like his father, since his asthma and hay fever had been misdiagnosed as tuberculosis.

In addition, he had just dropped out of Harvard University, giving up his quest for a degree after two years. This was his second and final attempt at higher education. Several years earlier he had attended Dartmouth College at Hanover, New Hampshire, but quit there after just two months. His disappointed grandfather could not understand his unambitious grandson, but gave him the farm in Derry hoping his kin could manage as a farmer.

Robert and Elinor had three more children born to them on the farm, and Frost did make a living of sorts, raising chickens and teaching part-time at Pinkerton Academy in Derry Village. But his mind was full of poetry. As time went on, he wrote more and farmed less, always

Robert Frost Farm Historic Site, Eric Sanford photograph.

encouraged by Elinor.

In 1911 Frost sold the farm and with the proceeds sailed for England with his wife and four children. He was unknown and virtually unpublished. In England he showed his poems to a London publisher, who printed his first two volumes of poetry, *A Boy's Will*, and *North To Boston*. They were quickly acclaimed on both sides of the Atlantic, and the previously unknown writer was hailed as the leader of "the new era in American poetry." When Frost returned to the United States in 1915, he faced sudden, unexpected, and lasting fame.

From then until his death in 1963 Frost wrote, read his poetry, stimulated generations of students, and received honors throughout the world. Four times he was awarded the Pulitzer Prize for poetry. The two-time college dropout received more than 50 honorary degrees, including ones from both Harvard and Dartmouth who were now eager to claim him as an alumnus.

Frost felt that the 10 years he spent at the Derry farm shaped the core of all his writing. It gave him two commodities important to a poet: time and seclusion. Although Frost later bought other farms (he once owned five at the same time) the Derry property held a special place in his heart. In later years when he traveled to New Hampshire he was appalled to find the house being used as a commercial garage with an auto junkyard spreading into the fields. He hoped to reclaim the property, but was unable to carry out the project.

The state of New Hampshire acquired the farm in 1965, and has since restored it to its condition at the turn of the century. In 1900 the house was a simple two-story white clapboard New England farmhouse about 20 years old. The poet's daughter, Lesley Frost

Ballantine, assured that the restoration was accurate. The dining room dishes are original, but most of the furnishings were selected to be representative of the few owned by the family, including a chair similar to the one Frost sat in each night as he wrote. There are family paintings and photographs. A short film gives views of the farm and grounds to a background of selected poetry readings.

On the grounds, the orchard, the barn, and the brook with its wildflowers —all reflected in Frost's works—have been restored. A short nature trail leads through the woods. And at the south end is the famous Mending Wall where Napoleon Guay and the poet labored each springtime.

The Robert Frost Farm Trustees help the state maintain the farm. It is open weekends beginning Memorial Day, and Wednesday through Sunday from late June through Labor Day. A fee is charged.

53 DANIEL WEBSTER BIRTHPLACE HISTORIC SITE

Franklin

Off N.H. Route 127, 1 mile south of Franklin

Daniel Webster, one of New Hampshire's best known native sons, was born January 18, 1782, in a two-room cabin in what is now the town of Franklin. At that time there were few white settlers between the Webster homestead and the Canadian border.

When the boy was two, the family moved to a nearby home with larger quarters. In 1797 he entered Dartmouth College in Hanover. In his junior year he gave the Fourth of July oration.

After studying law in Boston, Massachusetts, Webster practiced law for

Daniel Webster Birthplace Historic Site, George Sylvester photograph.

several years in Boscawen, just south of Franklin, and moved to Portsmouth in 1807. Although he was elected to the United States Congress from Portsmouth, greater opportunity lured him to Boston. His skill and talent as an orator were much in demand, making him one of the highest paid lawyers of his time. He served two terms as Congressman from Boston, four terms as United States Senator, and was Secretary of State under three presidents. He died while Secretary of State in 1852.

Many of Webster's speeches had decisive effects on national life. His arguments in the Dartmouth College case stopped the New Hampshire legislature from rescinding his alma mater's charter, thus maintaining the system of private colleges and institutions that still exists today. His famous "Seventh of March" oration in 1850 before the United States Senate defended Henry Clay's Missouri Compromise, even though he and Clay were political enemies. The compromise allowed for California's admission as a free state, but made no provision for new land to be either free or slave territory. Many felt that this controversial speech later cost Webster a presidential nomination.

In 1904 Webster's birthplace was purchased by Arthur C. Jackson, and the Daniel Webster Birth Place Association was formed. Jackson planned to move the cabin west to the St. Louis Exposition that summer. But this was vetoed by the bank, Franklin Building and Loan Association, who foreclosed on the mortgage. The Franklin Board of Trade organized to save the birthplace, and in 1909 the restored building was opened to the public. In 1917 it was deeded to the state of New Hampshire. Today the Division of Parks manages 20 of the 150 acres of Ebenezer Webster's farm.

The birthplace today is a compromise restoration of the original building, which was an ell or extension of the main house. Original brickwork and foundation were used as much as possible, so that the big fireplace, hearth, and iron kettle closely approximate the original. There are period type furnishings, some original family dishes, and Daniel Webster's life insurance policy. The old barn is being renovated and converted to a seasonal theater, with a planned opening of July, 1985.

The birthplace is open from Memorial Day to Labor Day, and a fee is charged.

Odiorne Point State Park, George Sylvester photograph.

SEACOAST REGION

Odiorne Point State Park, George Sylvester photograph.

54 ODIORNE POINT STATE PARK
Rye

On N.H. Route 1A

New Hampshire's coastline stretches a brief 18 miles between the borders of Maine and Massachusetts. Most of the shoreline itself, and the inner tidal marsh or lagoon, is publicly owned, and protected from development. But for better or worse, the shoreline and tidal marsh are usually separated by an unbroken stretch of motels, houses, restaurants, and amusement centers.

The last, and only sizeable undeveloped piece of New Hampshire's tidal and marsh ecology — with no intervening development — lies within the 137 protected and unique acres of Odiorne Point State Park.

Odiorne Point, just outside of Portsmouth Harbor, was the site of the first permanent settlement in New Hampshire when David Thomson established a trading center in 1623. Although Thomson left a few years later, other settlers remained. In 1660 John Odiorne purchased a homestead area, which remained in the family for 282 years. Over the years the land has been used for farming, as a summer resort (the Sagamore House, which burned to the ground in 1871), and for large seaside estates.

Paradoxically it was World War II and the threat of enemy attack that prevented further development of the area and led to the present park. Following Pearl Harbor in late 1941, Odiorne

Point was comandeered by the U.S. Army to protect Portsmouth Harbor with its vital naval shipyard. On short notice, residents were forced to vacate their farms and homes. Giant 16-inch guns and batteries of 155-millimeter anti-aircraft cannon were emplaced throughout the former family estates.

The base, which never saw action, was named Fort Dearborn to honor General Henry Dearborn. Born in Hampton, New Hampshire, in 1751, General Dearborn fought in the battle of Bunker Hill, Valley Forge, and in the War of 1812.

Following World War II, Fort Dearborn was partly dismantled, and used by the National Guard and Air Force as a radar site. Later declared surplus, it was sold to the state of New Hampshire in 1961 on condition it be developed as a state park.

Development has been slow, with an emphasis on preservation and interpretation. Today concrete casements and dirt-covered bunkers are all that remain of the Army days. Several miles of trail, including a marked nature trail, wind along the rocky, gently rolling shore, past pebble beaches, tidal marshes, and stands of Scotch pine, oak, shrubbery, and wild roses. Ubiquitous gulls soar overhead, as killdeer and wading birds feed in the tidal wash.

Picnic tables near the parking lot look out over the Atlantic to the granite Isles of Shoals, six miles offshore. The bunkers, camouflaged with dirt and trees by the Army, now function as shaded observation points. There is a bike path, and, at Seavey Creek, a boat launching site.

The Russell B. Tobey Visitor Center also houses a nature center. Accessible to the handicapped, the nature center is maintained cooperatively by the New Hampshire Division of Parks, the University of New Hampshire Sea Grant Marine Advisory Program, and the New Hampshire Audubon Society. Exhibits, illustrated talks, and guided walks are conducted during the summer months, with year-round programs for local school children. Scientists conduct research in marine biology and tidal ecology. The Friends of Odiorne Point, Inc. help the Division of Parks maintain the property.

The park is open all year. A fee is charged during the main season, June through September.

Rye Harbor State Park, George Sylvester photograph.

71

55 RYE HARBOR STATE PARK
Rye

On N.H. Route 1A

On Ragged Neck peninsula, this rocky ocean point overlooks picturesque Rye Harbor on the Atlantic Ocean. A rock jetty, ideal for salt water fishing or sightseeing, extends two hundred feet into the water. On clear days the Isles of Shoals can be seen on the horizon. The nearby picnic area is cooled by summer breezes.

At the harbor is a public dock, boat ramp, and a large mooring area. If you don't have your own boat to launch, you can get a ticket on one for a day of deep sea fishing, or just go for a short ocean sightseeing tour. Since the enactment of the 200-mile off-shore limit for foreign fishing vessels, commercial fishing has increased, and many large boats unload their catch here.

The main summer season runs from mid-June to mid-September. Fees are charged for picnicking and use of the boat ramp.

Rye Harbor State Park, George Sylvester photograph.

Hampton Beach State Beach, George Sylvester photograph.

56 HAMPTON STATE BEACH AND HARBOR

Hampton

Along N.H. Route 1A

Hampton Beach on the Atlantic Ocean has been a popular resort since the late 1800s. In those days it lay on the line for trolley cars from the Boston suburbs, an hour's run away. The tracks and the trolleys are gone, but hundreds of thousands of visitors pour in each year, seeking the gleaming sun and sand and ocean waves of one of New England's oldest and busiest seaside resorts.

Hampton State Beach and Harbor is the southernmost of several state-owned beaches and parks extending northward along New Hampshire's 18-mile coastline. Separated by small stretches of private or town-owned properties, the beaches preserve and protect a unique environment.

The 2,800-foot wide, sandy beach has a gradual underwater gradient for safe bathing. In addition to ocean bathing and beach activities, there are lifeguard services, a bathhouse with showers, a refreshment stand, and ample parking. Dogs are not permitted on the beach.

Under protection is one of the few remaining sand dune formations in the state. A rock jetty breakwater, accessible to visitors, juts several hundred feet into the Atlantic. The jetty protects adjacent Hampton Harbor from the pounding waves. Boats can be launched by the edge of the harbor from the state-owned pier.

The season extends from June through Labor Day. Fees are charged for parking and use of the bathhouse.

Marine Memorial, Hampton Central State Beach, George Sylvester photograph.

57 HAMPTON CENTRAL STATE BEACH
Hampton

Along N.H. Route 1A

Hampton Central Beach, in the center of the resort section, is best known for the Sea Shell, a state-owned amphitheater and band-shell. The Hampton Beach Chamber of Commerce holds free concerts several nights weekly in summer, with frequent special events such as fireworks and talent shows. The Sea Shell is provided with comfort stations, first aid, public information services, and observation points overlooking the ocean.

In addition to the Sea Shell, the state-owned portion of the beach extends north along the ocean for three miles for bathing and beach activities.

All the facilities of a major resort are available in town, virtually across the street from the park.

On the beach is the New Hampshire Marine Memorial, a granite statue of a woman gazing mournfully out to sea. Designed by the late Alice Cosgrove, the shrine memorializes New Hampshire sons and daughters who gave up their lives at sea in the service of their country.

Parking is metered. The season extends from May through Labor Day.

58 JENNESS STATE BEACH

Rye

On N.H. Route 1A

Jenness State Beach stretches for about a half-mile along the Atlantic Ocean. Facilities are limited to a small parking area and a restroom and changing area. Picnic sites are available at Rye Harbor, or 3 miles north at Odiorne Point State Park. Shops, restaurants, and motels are located across the street.

Parking is metered. The beach is open from early May to mid-September.

59 NORTH BEACH STATE BEACH

Hampton

On N.H. Route 1A

North Beach extends for about a mile and a half along the ocean north from Great Boar's Head to the junction of Routes 1A and 101C. Although the beach is narrow in places, there are many stretches of smooth, packed sand.

A sea wall separates the beach from the busy highway. When conditions are right, the surf crashes against the sea wall, often washing over to the highway.

Facilities are limited to a small comfort station at the north end. Parking is metered. The season extends from June through Labor Day.

60 NORTH HAMPTON STATE BEACH

North Hampton

On N.H. Route 1A

North Hampton State Beach features 1,000 feet of sandy beach on the ocean. Restrooms and changing facilities are on site. Metered parking is available at the beach's edge. There are no picnic facilities, and fires are not permitted. However, refreshments are available in town across the street.

The beach is open from May to mid-September. Parking is metered.

61 WALLIS SANDS STATE BEACH

Rye

On N.H. Route 1A

New Hampshire's coastline is only 18 miles long, but much of it is in public ownership. Wallis Sands State Beach preserves one of the state's finest beaches.

This popular park covers only 18 acres. It provides ocean bathing on a pristine 800-foot long sandy beach. A bathhouse with showers gives easy access to the beach, which is 150 feet wide at high tide. There is plenty of parking close to the beach, and a convenient refreshment stand. For early risers sunrise over the Atlantic can be spectacular, with the Isles of Shoals on the horizon in the background.

The bathing season begins weekends in mid-May, and runs daily from mid-June to Labor Day. Crowds can be heavy on summer weekends. A combined fee covers parking, bathhouse facilities, and use of the beach.

62 FORT CONSTITUTION HISTORIC SITE

New Castle

On N.H. Route 1B at U.S. Coast Guard Station

Fort Constitution at the mouth of the Piscataqua River preserves a military history going back more than 350 years. In 1632, the British, well aware of the need to defend Portsmouth Harbor, installed four guns in an earthwork fort on the site. During the French and Indian Wars in 1666, a timber blockhouse was built. The fort, one of several units along the coast, was named Castle William and Mary in honor of England's reigning monarchs.

The most dramatic role of the fort came on December 13, 1774, the eve of the American Revolution. This was four months before Paul Revere's famous ride which lead to the Battle of Lexington and Concord. On this December night Paul Revere was making another ride, bringing the message to New Castle that the fort at Rhode Island was destroyed, and that British troops were coming to take over William and Mary. The next day steady drum beats rolled over the water of the Piscataqua, summoning the Sons of Liberty from Portsmouth, Rye, New Castle, Durham, and other nearby towns. Four hundred patriots overpowered the small British force, removing five tons of gunpowder, 16 cannons, and other military hardware. This was the first open act against the King, four months before the actual Revolution began.

Royal Governor John Wentworth sent to Boston for help, and two ships with 100 British marines and 40 guns were deployed. The raids stopped, but tension remained high.

Fort Constitution Historic Site, George Sylvester photograph.

In 1791 the new state of New Hampshire gave the fort and lighthouse to the United States. Renamed Fort Constitution, it was renovated in 1808 with taller walls and brick buildings, and used during the War of 1812. It is the ruins of this fort that visitors see today.

At the time of the Civil War, it was planned to build a more massive masonry fort, but with the advent of steam, heavily armed warships made such masonry forts obsolete.

Mine laying and storage equipment was installed in 1897 and 1903 in the area now occupied by the Coast Guard. These were used during the Spanish American War and both World War I and World War II when mines were placed in Portsmouth Harbor. In 1961 Fort Constitution was returned to the state. It was placed on the National Register of Historic Places in 1973.

Today all that remains of the 17th century fort is the base of the walls. Much can be seen of the 1808 construction, including the restored portcullis and gateway, powder magazine, ramp for moving guns, and the terreplain platform for firing the batteries. Foundation, sites, and remnants of both earlier and later construction can be seen.

Adjacent to the historic site are the picturesque Portsmouth Harbor lighthouse and United States Coast Guard station where modern cutters are usually berthed. This is the latest military installation in an unbroken line going back to 1632.

The site is open all year. A fee is charged on weekends and holidays.

63 FORT STARK HISTORIC SITE

New Castle

At the end of Wild Rose Lane

Fort Stark, overlooking Portsmouth Harbor and the mouth of the Piscataqua River, was first used as a fort in 1746. Because it has been used in every war from the Revolution through World War II, the 10-acre site shows many changes in military architecture and technology.

The first permanent fort was built in 1775, to be followed by the earth and timber First System Fort in 1794. Further modifications were constructed for the War of 1812.

In the early 1900s the site was named to memorialize John Stark, New Hampshire's commander during the Battle of Bennington, and the fort became the back-up post for Fort Dearborn (now Odiorne Point State Park).

When World War II loomed on the horizon in 1941, the fort served as the Harbor Entrance Control Post for the entire Portsmouth Harbor defense area.

The communication center, which resembles the upper half of a battleship, can still be visited today. In addition, there are remnants of batteries and other structures.

In addition to the fort's military significance, there are spectacular views of the ocean, Odiorne Point State Park, Little Harbor, and the nearby Maine coast, with shore walks along the sandy and rocky shore.

The final parcel of the fort was obtained in 1983, and development is still under way. There are no restrooms or parking facilities. The walk system is unfinished, and there are unprotected stairs, high walls, and rough ground. Because of this, visitors should exercise caution, and there is no access for the handicapped.

Fort Stark is open weekends and holidays only from Memorial Day to Labor Day. A fee is charged.

Wentworth-Coolidge Mansion Historic Site, George Sylvester photograph.

64 WENTWORTH-COOLIDGE MANSION HISTORIC SITE
Portsmouth

At the end of Little Harbor Road, two miles from downtown Portsmouth off N.H. Route 1A

Portsmouth was the hub of New Hampshire in the 1700s, an important seaport and commercial center. Wealth and fashion were at their height, with many stately dwellings reflecting the aristocratic life of the community. A center of this activity was the 40-room mansion of Royal Governor Benning Wentworth.

King George II commissioned Wentworth as royal governor in 1741 when the province of New Hampshire was separated from Massachusetts. Wentworth was then 46 years old. Reappointed by King George III, he

served until 1766, longer than any other royal governor in America. During his 25-year tenure he granted more territory and new townships than any of his predecessors. For each land grant the royal governor received a handsome fee, plus a 500-acre lot from the grant. New Hampshire was prospering, and so was Wentworth, who eventually acquired some 100,000 acres widely dispersed over the territory.

But he slowly grew in disfavor with the crown. This reached a peak when he issued grants for more than 60 townships across the Connecticut River out of his jurisdiction. Public outcry demanded his removal, and in 1766 at age 71, he resigned. He lived in the mansion in retirement until his death in 1770.

From the outside the mansion has a rambling appearance, with extensions seemingly stuck on randomly. Like many early buildings, it actually is a composite, reflecting five distinct periods in construction. Originally it was a small fisherman's cottage, built around 1695. It was enlarged in the early 1700s by Benning Wentworth's grandfather. But it received its most extensive renovations in 1750 after Wentworth inherited it and added its most elegant features.

The house, and Wentworth's marriage, was memorialized with some poetic license by Longfellow in his *Tales of a Wayside Inn*. In fact, during the governor's 60th birthday dinner he amazed his guests when he unexpectedly married his youthful and lithesome housekeeper.

Following Wentworth's death his widow remarried and remained at the estate with her second husband. In 1789 she served tea to George Washington and his staff. After her death the house passed through several owners until it was acquired by John Templeman Coolidge, a prominent Boston artist and trustee of the Boston Museum of Fine Arts. It remained in his family until the mid-1950s when his widow offered the mansion to the state. It was renovated in 1966, and is now partially furnished.

The craftsmanship of the Portsmouth shipbuilders is reflected throughout the 40 rooms. Many have exposed beams, gunstock corners, wide board floors, and detailed woodwork. Most impressive is the Council Chamber, scene of many a turbulent meeting in pre-Revolutionary days. The huge fireplace and magnificent chimney wall are flanked by carvings reminiscent of a ship's figurehead. Many rooms have cut paneled doors, wainscoting, and even wallpaper imported from France in the 1750s. Off the waiting room is a hidden "spy room" where aides checked out visitors who came to call on the governor. They arrived by coach or by water, tying up at the governor's private dock.

The mansion is considered one of the most magnificent of the Colonial era. It is open weekends beginning Memorial Day, and daily from late June to Labor Day. A fee is charged.

Index

About the Author

Bruce Sloane first began visiting New Hampshire state parks when he was an undergraduate student at Dartmouth College in Hanover. After getting a master of science degree in geology from Montana State University, he worked as a park ranger with the National Park Service in Carlsbad Caverns, Petrified Forest, Virgin Islands, and Everglades National Parks.

Today Bruce lives in Boscawen in a 200-year old house with three chimneys, four fireplaces and a barn. Living with him are his wife, two daughters, two cats, and a dog. His previous book, *Cavers, Caves, and Caving,* was published by Rutgers University Press.

He is employed as a technical writer by Digital Equipment Corporation in Merrimack.